T0194573

THE MASTER'S KEY

BECOMING THE KEY TO UNLOCKING
GOD'S PURPOSE FOR YOUR LIFE

J. J. MIDDAGH

WESTBOW
PRESS®
A DIVISION OF THOMAS NELSON
& ZONDERVAN

WestBow Press books may be ordered through booksellers or by contacting:

WestBow Press
A Division of Thomas Nelson & Zondervan
1663 Liberty Drive
Bloomington, IN 47403
www.westbowpress.com
1 (866) 928-1240

ISBN: 978-1-9736-4799-7 (sc)
ISBN: 978-1-9736-4798-0 (hc)
ISBN: 978-1-9736-4800-0 (e)

Library of Congress Control Number: 2018914443

Print information available on the last page.

WestBow Press rev. date: 07/31/2019

Contents

I will give you the keys of the kingdom of heaven; whatever you bind on earth will be bound in heaven, and whatever you loose on earth will be loosed in heaven.

—Matthew 16:19 (NIV)

To Dad.

Unlocked the world you did.

Key \kē\

adjective

1. of paramount or crucial importance.

Chapter 1
KEY

I OPENED THE DRAWER in the kitchen and riffled through my collection of life's paraphernalia. Stamps, business cards, magnets, and every other imaginable thing rattled around as I sifted through the contents of the drawer, searching for a proverbial needle in this haystack. Finally, I caught a glimpse of what I sought. The glinting surface reflecting the kitchen light was an instant giveaway. The key I needed to unlock an old file cabinet sat there mocking me like a child after a protracted game of hide-and-seek.

I picked up the key and headed to the filing cabinet. A breath of anticipation passed from my lungs as I got closer, excited about the treasures that lay therein. My excitement was attributed to my ability to remember where I had placed the key. I was able to find it despite how obviously disorganized this drawer was.

When I reached the filing cabinet, I quickly inserted the key and was immediately deflated. The key didn't fit. *It must be upside down*, I thought. *I'll flip it and try again.*

Same result. The key wouldn't even enter the keyhole. I tried again and again, rejected each time as if I were some kid trying to ride a roller coaster, but the signs kept declaring I was an inch too short.

It's interesting how we fall into acts of insanity to somehow overcome a blow to our pride. In this situation, either this was not the right key or I was incapable of using the key correctly. Either way, my pride was not walking away untarnished.

I knew this was the key to the filing cabinet. It was exactly where I had placed it, it looked just like it, and it even felt like the key I remembered using to open the cabinet before. Therefore, it had to be the key.

It became clear how much I didn't want to be wrong about the key. I didn't want to be defeated by a key. What began to haunt my mind, one creeping thought at a time, was the realization that if this wasn't the key, then where was it?

Despite my best efforts to extinguish those dark thoughts, doubt overcame my mind. My focus shifted from attempting to shove the key into the keyhole, repeating the same steps over and over again while expecting some alternative outcome, to eventually addressing the problem of where I could find the correct key.

I leaned my forehead against the filing cabinet in defeat and surrendered, bested by a key. If this wasn't the key, then what did this key open? I closed my eyes and thought, *Did my wife move the key? Did the key get thrown away by accident?*

Then panic set in.

What if I can't open the filing cabinet? How embarrassing is it to call a locksmith for a filing cabinet? What else is in the filing cabinet?

THE SOMEDAY DRAWER

Every place I have lived has had a junk drawer. Despite my best efforts to eliminate mess and clutter, a drawer full of forgotten pieces of life always seems to return. I am not sure what percentage of families have a junk drawer somewhere in their homes, but in my experience, everyone has at least one. The items in these drawers are categorized as those things that may offer some purpose in our lives, just not in this immediate moment.

Most of the business cards, magnets, markers, and keys in my junk drawer have a purpose. I think I will rename it "the someday drawer." It has a better ring to it, and it reduces my anxiety about being disorganized.

The one thing I noticed about my someday drawer is that it has quite a few keys in it. I can't honestly tell you what all of them open, but I found it interesting how many were there. I have a prominent and handy key hanger in my house. My wife hung it in the closet near the garage door for us to hang our keys on. This made me think, *Why aren't all my keys on the key hanger?*

The answer is obvious. Not all keys share the same significance. Some keys we use every day, while others we use once a week, once a month, or even once a year. Apparently, in our house, the keys that are not used on a regular basis are relegated to the someday drawer, while the keys we use every day are hung on the key hanger as if they were trophies, displayed for all to see.

Keys, by definition, are important. They provide the means to unlock something, typically something valuable. Regardless of where the key ends up, it still has a purpose. Without it, there is a lock somewhere that will remain unopened.

KEYS

Keys manifest in many ways. The key to my car is different from the key to my house or even my mailbox. Each key is crafted and designed for a specific lock, with a specific purpose. Some keys put objects into motion. That is, they bring something to life (e.g., a car). Other keys provide access to items or places that are designed to be secure. Keys are intended to be unique, though this is not to say keys can never be the same.

It is not uncommon for a manufacturer to include more than one key as a form of redundancy to ensure that if one is lost, the other can take its place. The point of a key is to be relatively unique. If all keys were the same, there wouldn't be much point in having one.

The process of making a key can be simple or complex. Some keys are crafted in mere minutes, while others may require several skilled individuals to fulfill their purpose. If you consider how keys have evolved over time, it is quite remarkable how different they are today from even fifty years ago.

The key to my car doesn't fit into anything. The car detects the key in my pocket and allows me to operate the car. When I get in the car without the key, I receive a warning on the console. "No Key Detected."

Another example is the key to my office. This key isn't anything like a key that would come to mind in the traditional sense. It's a plastic card with a chip that is read by a scanner on the door, allowing me access to the building.

Some keys aren't even tangible. The passwords and PIN codes we enter into websites and programs each day are also keys that allow us access to those systems.

The point is keys aren't always of a specific shape and size. They often manifest differently based on their function.

MASTER KEY

People have quite a bit in common with keys. We all come from different backgrounds. We look different. We each have unique capabilities. Some of us are gifted with creative talents, and others with physical skills. Each of us comes into this world with the potential to unlock something.

What makes us different from most keys is that we have the ability to unlock an unlimited number of opportunities. We can open doors to educational opportunities, career opportunities, and even social opportunities. Throughout our lives, we are placed in situations where opportunities present themselves, and it is up to us to be the keys to unlock that potential.

As individuals, we are capable of amazing things. As such, through our trials and our experience, we become keys to open more opportunities. These capabilities bring us closer to becoming master keys for our lives—or in this case, the master's keys.

God has a purpose for everything in his creation. He began the universe with an intention, and each creation that followed thereafter was meant to fulfill his purpose. This includes your life and your purpose. You were chosen before the dawn of time to fulfill God's purpose for his kingdom and his creation. Paul said, "He chose us in him before the foundation of the world, that we would be holy and blameless before him in love" (Ephesians 1:4 NASB).

Within you is God's plan. Each season of your life is part of the process that molds you into the key to unlock his purpose for your life. Throughout history, we have been witnesses to people who became the key that was needed in the moment to reveal God's glory and propel his plans forward.

The Bible provides us with the account of people who became God's key in the moment to fulfill his plans. Moses, Joseph, Mary,

Paul, and many others were all prepared to be the keys to unlock their purposes in God's plan. What is remarkable about these stories is that we are provided not only the details of what each of them did for the kingdom of God but also how each of them was forged through trials, tragedies, and victories to fulfill God's plans.

We are fortunate to have these character accounts as we struggle through our own salvation with fear and trembling, being forged through our own trials and tribulations to become the keys to unlock God's purpose for our lives.

GOD'S PURPOSE

Purpose is a concept that many people wrestle with, regardless of what season they might be in in their lives. Not everyone encounters his or her purpose at a young age. For some, it may happen at middle age or even older. However, everyone is born with a purpose.

Solomon describes it in this way: "The purposes of a person's heart are deep waters, but one who has insight draws them out" (Proverbs 20:5 NIV). I find it interesting that Solomon refers to purpose as being associated with a person's heart. Jesus later emphasizes that a person's heart is what matters. God gave us each a purpose, and he provides a lifetime of trial and error to reveal it and a plethora of opportunities to fulfill it.

Purpose for each of us can be subjective. God grants us free will to attempt to fulfill whatever purpose we desire. Subjective purpose is the purpose we seek for ourselves. A subjective purpose may or may not be part of God's plan. So, the question you may be asking is, How do you know if your subjective purpose aligns with God's purpose for your life? This can be a difficult question to answer, but it doesn't have to be.

We have already established that the purpose of a person's heart is revealed only with insight. Only through wisdom can a person's true purpose be revealed. God's purpose for your life isn't always what makes you feel good. It's not always what makes you comfortable. More often than not, God's purpose for our lives will place us outside of our comfort zone. We will see more of this later in the chapters that follow. Forging keys is not graceful or done in the absence of resistance. God seeks to carve and etch each piece of us to become the key he wants in order to fulfill his purpose.

If you consider some of the individuals our culture sees as spiritual heroes, it can seem daunting, as if somehow we have to measure up to people like Billy Graham or Mother Teresa. Let's not even begin to consider the stories and sacrifices of many of the characters in the Bible.

Comparing ourselves to these spiritual giants can make revealing our purpose seem difficult or trivial. Studying these people, however, is not about becoming them. It's about understanding how God intervenes and presents situations and circumstances that many of us can relate to.

Mother Teresa spoke of hearing God's voice from the time she was a little girl. In witnessing the suffering of others, she chose to dedicate her life to God. She also explained that not long after becoming a nun, the voice stopped. She was confused, frustrated, and disappointed (Martin 2015). It didn't make sense that God's voice would vanish after she committed herself to him.

Her desire to be closer to God was tied to her life's work. The need to experience the closeness she felt to God when she heard his voice motivated her to continue her work. She spent a lifetime caring for orphans and those who were less fortunate. She worked her entire life to hear that voice again. It makes one wonder how hard she would have worked had she continued to hear the voice all along.

God knew Mother Teresa; he knew she would be driven to fulfill his plans just to hear his voice again. As difficult as this was for Mother Teresa, consider how many lives she changed as a result. This is just one example of how God's purpose can manifest for someone.

Remember, the key is not to think that God has called us to be Mother Teresa; it's to understand that God presents us with opportunities to become exactly what he needs us to be. The hard part is that when God presents those opportunities, we need to be ready to listen.

LISTENING

If you grew up in a family like I did, you are no stranger to being told to listen. "Clean out your ears!" my father used to say. I remember being taken to the doctor for a hearing exam. According to the doctor, I had superhuman hearing. My parents were stunned because they were certain I was partially deaf. The doctor explained that I didn't have a hearing problem, but I did have a listening problem. All of us run into this same situation when it comes to God.

God's involvement in our lives often manifests as a sense of being nudged in one direction or another. We are all too often distracted by the stuff of this world to notice his guidance, and as a result, we may dismiss it. Our culture trains us to dismiss it.

We are constantly being told to do what feels good, to seek after what we want, that it's our world, that we should make it about us. Letting go of these beliefs and surrendering the pieces of us that matter in the moment is often difficult and, in some cases, requires surgery on our spirit before we can truly let go. You may feel like you need to let go of a relationship, or a job, or maybe distance yourself from a family member.

All of these decisions can be difficult. Our heart tells us one thing; our mind tells us another. "The heart of man plans his way, but the Lord establishes his steps" (Proverbs 16:9 ESV). This verse reveals that it is our nature to look to our hearts for the plans we have, and it is God who provides us with the means to get there.

When it comes to listening to God, I cannot emphasize enough the significance of prayer in revealing God's plan for your life. God doesn't want you to think you are the center of the universe. He wants you to understand that you are at the center of his heart. The time you have here is so small compared to the time you will have with him. Seek his plans first and watch the life he has planned for you become revealed.

DOING

When I was in high school, my father gave me a book that I dismissed quickly. The book *Do It! Let's Get Off Our Buts* by Peter McWilliams echoed the "Just Do It" slogans and can-do attitude that had begun to permeate society in the 1990s. In the book, McWilliams encourages his audience to stop making excuses and start taking action. He calls out his readers' incessant ability to make statements such as "I would go to law school but, but ..." I noticed quickly that I was no stranger to these types of statements, allowing one too many "buts" to get in the way of achieving my goals.

I may have misspoken earlier in this chapter when I stated that listening is the hard part. That's not entirely accurate. Doing can make listening look like a lazy afternoon on a park bench. There are many chapters in the Bible that encourage readers to take action. One verse that comes to mind calls out the reader, not unlike Peter McWilliams did in his book. "But the one who looks into the perfect law, the law of liberty, and perseveres, being no hearer who forgets but a doer who acts, he will be blessed in his doing" (James 1:23–25 ESV). James called his audience to action. How many times have you heard "Faith without works is dead" (James 2:26 NASB)? James again called on his readers to act out their faith for others. When it comes to purpose, the doing is where the going gets tough.

All too often, doing is far more terrifying than listening. Why is it that God calls us to do things that seem reckless and negligent? Let's take some examples from the Bible—Abraham being asked to sacrifice Isaac, Moses leading God's people into the wilderness, Daniel being offered up as feline fancy, David going up against a man mountain, and Peter being asked to walk on water. All of these examples are actions that anyone of us would only be considered categorically sane for refusing to participate! So, what is going on in all these examples? Why is God revealing his purpose with such difficult, seemingly impossible actions? It has to do with reliance on God.

In the sixth chapter of Daniel, we are witness to a story of commitment and faith. Daniel, a good and faithful prophet of God, is challenged by a decree that would require his daily prayers to cease. The decree includes the consequence of death for any who violate this ordinance. Upon hearing this decree, what does Daniel do? What would you do? Relocate, hide, or pray in some place where no one will see you? Not Daniel. Upon hearing of the decree, Daniel retreated to prayer. He didn't even change the venue or the format. The scripture tells us that Daniel opened the windows toward Jerusalem, got down on his knees, and prayed three times a day, "just as he had done before" (Daniel 6:10 NIV). This is one of the purest examples of how we become formed by God for his purpose.

When the free will of others threatens our way life or our existence, we are called to do what Daniel did. Pray. Daniel surrendered to his circumstances. Stopping his relationship with God was not an option. The decree of the king was not going to change. This left Daniel with only one option—surrendering the circumstance to his father and relying on him that his will be done. Daniel had the faith to do something incredible, to take a chance, to leave the safety of his life and the outcome of his circumstances to an almighty and loving God.

The doing God asks of us, which we carry out in faith, always requires us to rely on him, just as Daniel relied on God when he opened those windows and got down on his knees. Our doubts can undermine our purpose, and when we begin to rely on ourselves, it's easy to begin to sabotage or even sacrifice our relationship with God. But just as Daniel cried out to his heavenly father as he entered the den of lions, it is important for us to cry out to God amid our circumstances. God answers our cries even in the midst of our doubts.

This is the business of doing. Being called to a purpose that requires a reliance on God is what we were made for. When it comes to revealing God's purpose for your life, leaps of faith come with the territory. I am not suggesting you go spend the night in your local zoo's lion exhibit or try wandering through the desert for forty years, or even attempt a water sprint at the local YMCA. What I am suggesting is that discovering God's purpose for your life may require a lot of faith and a little bit of getting off your butt.

You may feel forgotten, thrown in the back of some drawer, no light shining on your surface, tucked under some business card that hides your true potential. Maybe you're stuck to some magnet that you are having a hard time breaking away from, knowing deep down that as long as you are stuck, you can never reach your full potential. The world wants to convince you that you belong among the meaningless, that your value is measured in comparison to everyone else's. This is not the case. If you look hard enough, it will become clear that all those sharp edges you have formed over a life filled with tragedy, joy, victory, and defeat are the characteristics you need to unlock your true purpose—a purpose for a master, a way to become a master key. Remember that in God's house there are no junk drawers; there are only someday drawers.

Chapter 2
PURPOSE

PURPOSE HAS ALWAYS been a squishy subject. Ask any person on the street what their purpose is, and you will get a plethora of answers. Many will speak about being good parents, others will talk about contributing to the greater good, and you may even find some who say there is no purpose. One of my assumptions, which encouraged me to write this book, is that all of us have a purpose. I would argue that existence is not without its own sense of implied function.

It would be difficult to persuade me that a creation so complex as humanity serves no purpose. Many would argue that, pragmatically speaking, the purpose of humanity is to perpetuate the species. I might be willing to accept that; however, if that were the case, why the complexity? Many species succeed at the aforementioned task in the absence of such convolutions as jealousy, love, rage, and self-reflection. This appears to have driven us to a familiar question of what separates humans from beasts. I say it's our unique purpose.

I have a small desk fan that sits next to my keyboard. It runs off a USB plug that conveniently connects to my computer. Nothing too fancy about it—no speed adjustment, and it doesn't even swivel. As a result, when I sit at my desk, my eyes are competing for the title of driest place on earth. Its purpose is concise: accelerate air from one place to another. Someone at Honeywell sat down with an intention in mind to accomplish such a task, and this is the result. Is it possible to decompose the purpose of humanity in a similar way?

Humans can be broken down into several functions. Humans gather information. We manipulate that information and store it for later use. Using different senses, we capture data about our environment, other people, and ourselves. That information is filtered through a rather complex and elaborate heuristic system of analytics and experience. It is then transformed and stored, making it available to be leveraged for future experience or interaction. The heuristic system and analytics are the parts that fascinate me.

If all you wanted to do as a creator was to have your creation propagate itself, why not eliminate this piece? If you think about it, that piece is what drove Adam and Eve to a decision that resulted in all of us keeping clothing stores in business. That same piece that prompted Cain to kill Abel, not to mention every murder that followed. If you stop and consider that God not only gave us this piece but *intended* to give it to us from the beginning, several questions will begin to flood your mind. *Why? To what end? For what purpose?* This piece from God is made up of freedom, choice, and spirit. It's a subtle superpower that we all possess, and it is intended to fulfill a super purpose.

What was Adam's purpose, and from where did it come? Adam's purpose was given to him by God.

> The Lord God took the man and put him in the
> Garden of Eden to work it and take care of it.
> Genesis (2:15 NIV)

A gardener and a zookeeper. Adam's job was to take care of the garden and the animals in the garden. Not a bad job. I mean, he had me at gardening. I love my garden; probably not as impressive as Eden, but I enjoy it.

I'd like to think Adam and I would have made great neighbors. Think of the gardening tips he could share. Probably would have competed over which garden is nicer.

Tending a garden and taking care of animals is a tall order. I can't even get my twelve-year-old to clean up after our German shepherd. It's apparent that this was no task Adam could do alone, and God challenges Adam with finding a suitable helper among his creations (Gen. 2:18). Adam was unable to find a suitable helper within God's creation (Gen. 2:20). God intervenes and creates the perfect helper for Adam when he creates Eve.

It is important to note that the Hebrew word here for suitable helper is עֵזֶר (ezer) כְּנֶגְדּוֹ (kenegdo) ("ay-zer," "ken-egg-do"). This phrase means "helper designed for him." Ezer is used in the Old Testament to denote moments of strong support or rescue (Freedman 1983). On several occasions throughout the Old Testament, this is the same word used to describe God as a helper (Walton 2001).

This word choice is deliberate in defining Eve's role and purpose. I often wonder if the reason God created Eve was not because Adam couldn't handle the garden but because he kept getting lost and refused to ask for directions. Adam and Eve in the garden together prompted another purpose—a purpose for humanity that could be fulfilled only if Adam and Eve coexisted.

> God blessed them and said to them, "Be fruitful
> and increase in number; fill the earth and subdue
> it. Rule over the fish in the sea and the birds in the
> sky and over every living creature that moves on the
> ground." (Genesis 1:28 NIV)

Now please don't misunderstand. I am not saying that Eve's purpose was to be barefoot and pregnant. Everything God intended for Adam and Eve was a shared responsibility, both tending the garden in addition to being fruitful and multiplying.

This shared purpose brings to the surface a necessity for Adam and Eve to care about what happens to each other. They both know they are unable to carry out God's purpose in the absence of the other. Adam refers to Eve as if she is part of him (Gen. 2:23). This statement provides us with a strong indication Adam cares about Eve. There is no doubt that Eve cares for Adam as well.

God commanded Adam not to eat from the tree (Gen. 2:16), and it is clear that Eve is aware of this commandment, as is evidenced by her recitation of it during the conversation with the serpent in the third chapter of Genesis. They shared in this responsibility of following God's command to not eat from the forbidden tree. God had a specific plan for Adam and Eve, which involved their lives being blessed by his purpose under his guidance.

LOVE IN PURPOSE

We often lose sight of our purpose as a result of the noise of life. I call it static. I'm sure you have sources of static in your own life. News, work, social media, and in some cases certain friends or family members can all provide distractions that keep us from seeing God's plan and purpose for our lives. I see these distractions as tools used by the enemy to keep us right where he wants us. The Bible provides a perfect example of this static in the conversation that Eve has in chapter 3 with the serpent.

It fascinates me that the downfall of humanity started with a conversation. A conversation that persuaded Eve to do something she was forbidden to do. Have you ever had a situation like that? Sometimes it's a conversation with a friend or a colleague, or maybe a family member that justifies your actions, or perhaps some inner dialogue that sabotages your purpose. Our conversations, whether with others or with ourselves, have a natural tendency to justify our bad decisions and rationalize our way out of good ones.

These are the kinds of conversations that blind us to the truth and take us on a path that robs us of God's blessings. We see this in many of the books of the Old Testament. God's purpose never becomes clearer than when we seek him in his Word and in our prayer. The harder you work on the relationship you have with your creator, the closer you get to his purpose for your life. The more you focus on the distractions in life, the further you are from the purpose he has for you.

The intention God has for humanity is relatively straightforward. It can be broken down into two purposes. First, he wanted a relationship with his creation, as we can see in his relationship with Adam, and second, he wanted Adam and Eve to care about something other than themselves.

This is echoed by Jesus when he conveys the two most important commandments in Matthew 22. Love God with all your heart, mind, and soul—emphasizing our relationship with God—and love your neighbor as yourself, emphasizing our relationship with others. By placing Adam and Eve as custodians over his creation, he created a symbiotic relationship that required them to care about the occupants of the garden and each other.

Being tasked with tending to the garden made them responsible for a creation that was alive; it changed and responded to their involvement. This is the cause and effect of creation, the give and take of responsibility for something other than ourselves.

One of the first responsibilities given to Adam is naming the animals. These were creatures he shared the garden with and no doubt formed a connection with. To name something is to know it. I would not be surprised if Adam and Eve formed relationships with the animals and plants in the garden.

I have a strong relationship with the Hong Kong orchid trees in my backyard as well as my German shepherd, Kona. Nothing comes more naturally to me than walking through my garden with humankind's best friend. It's interesting that when I'm in my garden with Kona, my mind immediately begins a conversation with God.

These relationships that I have, and no doubt Adam and Eve had, were designed to coincide with God's purpose for humanity. This lesson in care and concern for the garden was elevated by Eve's arrival. Adam and Eve form a bond in their shared purpose, a purpose ordained by God and designed as a lesson in love, first for God and his creation and then for each other.

DIVINE TRAIN

Throughout the Bible, one thing is abundantly clear: God has a purpose, an intention for all he does and for all he allows. I think agenda, however appropriate, seems harsh in these circumstances, but we'll go with that. Think of God's will as a train lumbering toward its destination. Big, billowing smoke pours from the stack. The dense forest and snowcapped mountains pass in the background. There are a number of people on this train, and all of them are able to do just about anything they want. These people interact with one another. They affect one another's lives. Their decisions can change the course of what happens inside the train but not where the train is going. Ultimately, whatever destination that train has is where the train will end up.

God's divine will is the same; he has a plan that will be fulfilled regardless of what humanity does. We see this plan communicated through scripture. Throughout the Bible, we see his divine train heading toward the final station. In Daniel, Isaiah, and Revelation, we see evidence for kingdoms that have come and gone, the Messiah, and the end of time. All of these are part of the will of God and either have been carried out or will be. God's will is righteous and unwavering. Not only are his plans intended for you, they are perfect in every way.

SWEET SPOT OF PURPOSE

If God's will is ordained and humanity has the ability to choose him or not, how does purpose play a part in any of this? It could be argued that humanity can go its own way, and God still gets his outcome. God doesn't need you for his divine plans. That's the best part. Just like Adam and Eve, he wants you and me to be a part of those plans. That's the beauty in his design; he has no need for subordinates but a relentless desire for a relationship with his creation.

Let's look at it this way. Consider you are twenty-two years old, and you have a plan to retire when you are fifty-five. This is a commitment you have made to yourself, and you will do whatever is necessary to see this plan become a reality. This is your will. You make decisions that coincide with that plan. You go to work for a company with a generous pension plan and set up a 401(k) and maybe an IRA.

Each decision you make is under the backdrop of your plan to retire at fifty-five. Let's say you meet someone. You really like this person. So, you share your plan of retiring at fifty-five with them. Can you retire at fifty-five without them? Absolutely. However, the journey to retiring at fifty-five is far more enjoyable when shared with someone you love rather than going through life alone. It could also be argued that being fifty-five, retired, and alone is not as enjoyable as being retired at fifty-five and sharing it with a family.

God has a journey for this universe and all that's in it. He wants us to be a part of it and his plan. He wants to share it with us—all the beauty and wonder of his creation. He gives each of us a choice to be a part of that design. Your retirement goal had rules in place to ensure success. You either directly or indirectly communicated those rules to anyone who is on that journey with you. These rules are there to ensure your success and the success of those involved. With God's will, he provides a set of rules or laws of how we can be a part of his plan. These laws are designed to protect our hearts and ensure we are prepared for the purpose he has for each of us.

We have talked about God's divine will and his laws that he has put in place to govern his creation. There is another component that exists within this relationship. He also gave each of us a will, an ability to revolt, rebel, throw temper tantrums, and reject him in every way possible. This is the subject of just about every book in the Bible. Our will and God's will are in many cases at odds with each other.

This is as a result of the "free" in "free will." In later chapters, we will discuss the necessity of freedom in our will as part of God's creation, but for now, assume that providing humanity with the freedom to choose is the best outcome—maybe not always in the moment, but when it comes to the divine will of God, there is no alternative. Each of us has our own free will. If you have any doubts about whether we have free will, spend some time with a three-year-old and a box of crayons and watch the beautiful pictures that free will can draw all over your living room walls.

The concept of human will is one of the first characteristics of humanity we are exposed to in the Bible. The task we discussed earlier about Adam assigning names to the animals in the garden is evidence of free choice (Gen. 2:19). This is the first good example we see of Adam "choosing" something on his own. The Midrash (ancient Hebrew commentary on the scriptures) goes as far as to say that not even the angels had the power to name the animals God had created.

This underscores the significance of the free will that God gave humanity. This is to say that the free will God gave humanity is in some way different or enhanced from the agency that even angels possess. Our free will is the prerequisite characteristic that grants us the ability to love. Yes, in the absence of free will, love is not possible. Let me say that again. If you and I do not have the freedom to choose or reject God, love cannot exist. We will discuss that more in another chapter. What is important is to realize that our will has the potential to fit nicely into God's divine will and his moral guidance. The sweet spot of purpose is when our will aligns with God's divine will and is executed within the confines of his laws.

SHAPING OUR WILL

I was a strong-willed child. My parents and I were often at odds about how often to take a shower or whether or not the area under my bed should be included in the definition of a clean room. I am still that way in some cases. My parents convinced me on the shower frequency, but I still hide things under my bed (don't tell my parents). My wife will tell you that I am stubborn, to which I respond, "Don't confuse stubborn with convicted." Spoken like a true strong-willed person. Sure, I can attribute my stubbornness to the long line of stubborn male figures that preceded me; in some ways, I like to think I'm just carrying the torch. Don't ask me how many times that torch has lit my pride on fire.

I have met many people who could be considered weak willed. They struggle with an entirely different set of problems that strong-willed people do. Regardless of strong or weak, stubborn or amiable, all of us have some will that exists in us. I am convinced the image God refers to when he speaks of making humankind in his own image is the will that each of us possesses. The power to acknowledge or deny, love or hate, obey or disobey makes us unique and that power is made available to us in the gift of free will. God granted us a piece of who he is, his nature, in providing each of us with free will.

From our first breath, our will begins to take shape. Through our environment, we begin to push our will against the confines of our families and our society. We test our boundaries, first of our bodies, then of our environment, and ultimately of our parents' patience. Each milestone grants us more access to the freedom ingredient in free will. Crawling to walking, babbling to talking, each achievement reveals to us more of this gift from an almighty God who relentlessly pursues after us. Our families begin the process of shaping that will, a shape that has the ability to ensure our survival and success in the life we have been given.

God works through the situations and circumstances in our lives to shape us in his own way, nudging, guiding, and whispering each day to reveal his purpose for us. Sometimes through joy, oftentimes through tragedy, we change and are formed into the key to unlock his purpose for our lives. In the chapters that follow, we will begin to see how God uses our success, our failure, our disobedience, and our pride to become exactly what he needs us to be. Wherever you are in your journey with God, if you are here as part of this creation, and breath still flows through your lungs, your purpose in God's kingdom isn't finished. He has plans for you, plans to prosper you, plans to give you hope and a future.

Chapter 3

TRAGEDY

T HE HALLWAY FELT quiet but busy at the same time. I remember feeling my pulse quicken as I looked for which hallway to follow to arrive at the destination of my greatest fear. My search was abruptly halted as a

> "It's hard to know you belong here. That your purpose lies amongst all this pain."
>
> —Tom Clancy's *The Division*

police officer turned the corner the same time I did. Evan, all six feet and 280 pounds of him, wearing his full uniform, stopped as he saw me and placed his hand on my shoulder. Evan was a friend I had known from high school and had lost touch with. He of all people was about to deliver the most devastating news of my life. As he squeezed my shoulder, with his eyes welling up, he said, "He didn't make it." I looked to the floor of the hospital and surrendered in that moment to a plan and a divine decision that made no sense and surpassed all reason. Perhaps the contradiction of such an event to my life plan could only be explained by divine intervention.

My response to Evan came hollow and with such evidence of my surrender.

"Okay."

We walked down the hallway to the emergency room where the vessel that my father once inhabited lay. Fear enveloped me like a sickness welling up in my stomach and then like a fire engulfing my entire being. I turned the corner and saw my mother sitting next to my father's body, a sheet gently draped over him. She looked up at me with tears in her eyes and pleaded, "What am I going to do now?" I walked over and placed my hand on her shoulder as she began to sob.

Two things immediately entered my mind. The first was, *What would my father do if he was me?* And that was followed by, *Watch me now, Dad.* Neither of these thoughts is where my mind should have been. I should have rejoiced in my grief (Job 1:21). I should have prayed in my devastation, and I should have realized that I wasn't alone.

My father had passed away from an irregular heartbeat that would not return to normal despite the doctor's best efforts. He was a vibrant, healthy, and athletic seventy-one-year-young man with a new lease on life when God called him home and he departed this life to be with his parents.

This event shook my entire world. I was a mess for years. He was my father, my confidant, my mentor, and—most importantly—my best friend. It became clear that the pain and grief we encounter at the loss of a loved one is directly proportionate to the significance they hold in our lives. I had elevated my father throughout my entire life to a position above all other things. Any and everything I did was to make him proud. Now that he was gone, the world felt empty and without purpose.

I remember thinking, *If I can't make my dad proud of what I do, then what's the point in doing anything?* This led to depression and anxiety that manifested throughout my body. I would have moments where I couldn't breathe. At night when I would try to sleep, I would be shocked awake by a sense I was falling into oblivion.

HEALING

My body's physiological and psychological response to my father's loss went on for years. Doctors couldn't help me. Medication was not a solution that made any sense to me. I went to neurologists, ENTs, cardiologists, physical therapists, and even psychologists. None of these professionals could help me. Finally, I realized I was in the state I was in because of me and my irresponsibility.

It wasn't my dad's fault. It wasn't my wife's fault—or even my job. Most importantly, I knew it wasn't God's fault. Part of me was grateful to God. I would rather see my dad go out in his prime than suffer through endless days of him not knowing who I am. I saw my father's early departure as mercy for me and ultimately for him.

None of this changed the fact that there was a dad-shaped void in my life. That brings us back to whose fault it was. It was mine. Now many of you will say, *You are not responsible. You are only human.* That's not the problem, nor does it negate my responsibility.

Cynthia Swindoll once said that she had read a book that challenged her to realize "You are not irresponsible because you are sick, you are sick because you are irresponsible." Hearing this made me realize that we are all responsible for what we say, do, and think. Most importantly, we are responsible for what priority we give to God in our lives.

I had placed my father in a position above God, and as a result, his departure left a void in my life, which led to a physiological response that generated numerous consequences. This tragedy revealed the lack of importance I had placed on my relationship with God. For that, I am eternally grateful.

Please don't misunderstand. God is not punishing me for what I have or haven't done. God had a plan and purpose for my father in my life, and I didn't follow that plan.

The reason for God's plan to place him above my father was to protect me from this very thing. God knows the story of our lives and the consequences that our free will and the free will of others will create. He challenges us to place him above the people in our lives in order to protect our hearts.

Loss of our loved ones was never part of God's plan. He knows how hard loss is and wants our emotional emphasis to be on him more than anyone who may depart this life. We have an account in the Gospel of John of how God intimately understands the effects of losing those we love.

During Lazarus's funeral, Jesus witnesses the heartache of all those in attendance. In chapter 11, verse 33, we are told of how Jesus was moved by those who mourned the loss of Lazarus, so much so that even Jesus himself wept (John 11:35). He was not mourning the death of Lazarus; he knew in a matter of moments his friend Lazarus would be back to his old shenanigans. He wept because of the heartache he saw in those left behind.

God cares about your loss, and he knows firsthand the void it can create—a void that can be filled with a promise of seeing those we have lost again in his final creation.

For me, even six years later, I am still working to place God front and center in every arena of my life. God chases after us, and when he is unable to get our attention, he often uses tragedy to scream our names. I can say this much: he got mine. I can say unequivocally

J. J. MIDDAGH

that my family and I are all the better for it, even in the absence of my dad.

Tragedy is inevitable in this life. Many of you have encountered tragedy that goes far beyond the death of a parent. When I was eleven years old, I watched my aunt and uncle bury their daughter before she could graduate high school, and at the time, I had no idea the depths of grief they must have endured at her passing. In college, a friend of mine died as the result of a drunk driver. I witnessed her parents grieve her loss, and they continue to grieve to this day.

Tragedy is never trivial. It is not predicated on any objective definition. It is always personal. Tragic events manifest differently for each of us, and the methods we use to endure them are just as diverse. Abuse, neglect, and many other life-altering events leave us feeling empty and alone. When tragedy enters our life, how are we to respond? Shaking our fists at the sky and screaming doesn't seem to work; believe me, I've tried. What if loss and tragedy have a purpose? Pain is the result of sin in this world, despite that God uses these events to shape us into the key to unlock our true potential.

ALPHA AND OMEGA

What if you could see the outcome of every decision you ever made before you made it? Let's just focus on the big ones. *Do I buy that house? What school should I send my kids to? Should I marry him or not?* What if each of these decisions, and many others you knew the result of each decision at the very beginning? Would you change your decisions? I know the answer to that question for me is often yes. I think about all the grief I have caused myself and others. If I had known at the beginning what the outcome would be, I never would have made those choices.

28

This is still thinking in terms of one outcome—the outcome I know of. The alternatives may have been just as bad or even worse. God sees the beginning, the end, and everything in between. He knew the outcome before time began. Sometimes the tragedies we endure are the way God prepares us for his purpose. Some will say that's not fair or question the justice in that. These are reasonable responses to God's allowing tragedy and suffering in our lives. Perhaps someone in scripture can shed some light on tragedy and God's purpose for it.

SERVANT

The book of Job holds a special place in my collection of knowledge. I never thought much about Job until I read the last few chapters. Job's story provides us a remarkable and detailed example of the purpose of tragedy in our lives. The Bible refers to Job as "blameless and upright" (Job 1:1 NKJV). He was a wealthy man who lived in the land of Uz (Job 1:1, 3).

The details provided about Job are enough to give us a distinct picture of what Job must have been like and what kind of life he led. Job had it all money, influence, family, and friends. I use the term "friends" loosely here, as we later encounter three of these so-called friends. I think stooges may be a better word. We will come back to the stooges later; for now, let's focus on the details of Job's life as it is provided in the scripture. Job is a servant of God. God himself referred to Job in this manner (Job 1:8 NKJV). Servant of God—what does that really mean?

Servants are typically identified by their commitments, their actions, and what I like to call the notion of God in their lives. By notion, I mean that everything they do, every word they speak, every action they take is first filtered through their relationship with God. Daniel provides us another great example of a servant of God.

He served God even when the consequences of doing so meant death. Esther is another great example of a servant of God as she risks her life to plead for the lives of God's people. She knew God had placed her in the right place at the right time to be his ambassador to the world.

> For if you remain silent at this time, relief and deliverance for the Jews will arise from another place, but you and your father's family will perish. And who knows but that you have come to royal position for such a time as this? (Esther 4:14)

These people sought God in every decision they made. When the situation or circumstances proved to be outside their control, they immediately sought God in prayer. Daniel, upon hearing that his prayers would be his death sentence, went and prayed (Daniel 6:10). Esther, before going before the king, fasted for three days with her maids and commanded her cousin to have all the Jews do the same (Esther 4:16).

Servants of God are characterized by their commitment and faith. Since it is their notion to place God first in all things, when tragedy strikes, their response is always the same, to seek God first.

Another characteristic often found in servants of God is that they have an enormous target tattooed across their souls. These people have large contracts issued by the enemy on them. The enemy pursues and attacks them at every turn. Job, Daniel, and Esther all had moments and even seasons where the enemy attacked every arena of their lives.

Consider that the closer you get to becoming the key to unlocking the purpose God has for you, the more of a threat you become to the enemy. When our lives are on autopilot, seeking the next greatest trend, the next post, the next episode of our favorite TV show, that is exactly where Satan wants us to be. We go through the motions in an ever-persistent Groundhog Day, unfulfilled and absent of any intention.

I've been there. I know what it is to get up, get ready for work, go to work, come home, make dinner, watch TV, and go to bed, only to get up and do it all over again. All for what? The answer is we do it out of fear. It's life on the rails. No risks. Like bowling with the guards up. We bounce our way down the lane hoping to get a strike.

Satan has mastered the art of delivering fear to every receptor we possess. Everywhere I turn, from TV shows to movies, from news to posts, from health warnings to advertising, we are scared into a life of submission. What does it take to overcome being immersed in that degree of fear? It takes knowing you are not alone.

KINGDOM COLLAPSE

Job is not immune to Satan's campaign on the servants of God. He is brought to the brink of collapse by the enemy. We build our lives toward a destination. Our faith, our family, our friends, and our careers are kingdoms we build throughout our lives. As we get older, that kingdom becomes larger and gains momentum as we move forward in time.

For some of us, that kingdom continues as intended. For others like Job, an event occurs, something so tragic, something so antithetical to the course of our lives that it causes our kingdom to collapse. We sit in the ruins of our lives in disbelief, praying to wake up from the nightmare. I know what kingdom collapse was for me.

I had plans for my future with my dad. I knew all the things we were going to do as I got older. Our relationship was better than ever and was only improving daily. My wife, my father, and I would get up, work out together, and go have coffee. We would sit around and "talk story" all the way into lunch. My kingdom was right where I had planned it to be. When I saw him collapse that day, I felt my entire kingdom collapse.

This is a situation many can relate to. Losing a spouse, a child, or for some even a job can have this degree of impact on their lives. Consider for a moment losing it all at the same time. Not just a child but ten children—all the hopes and dreams you have for them gone in a flash.

The sounds of laughter are gone from your ears but haunt your mind. The smiles that once greeted you are now but a memory you desperately cling to, as if you know those images will fade from your mind if you don't burn them into your memories. You have the fear of forgetting them, what their voices sounded like, how they moved, how they smelled.

All of these things become a responsibility, as if you have now been appointed a keeper of their memory. It's a big job and one that brings you pain with every beat of your heart.

This is the situation Job finds himself in. Burying his children amid losing all his wealth. What does a servant of God do when everything he ever cared for is gone? If you're Job, you worship.

RESPOND

In the first chapter of Job, we get an eye-witness account of Job's response to being a penniless, fatherless, and destitute man.

> Then Job arose, tore his robe, and shaved his head; and he fell to the ground and worshiped. And he said: "Naked I came from my mother's womb, and

naked shall I return there. The Lord gave, and the Lord has taken away; Blessed be the name of the Lord." (Job 1:20–21 NKJV)

Job worshipped God in this moment. His grief is evident by the tearing of his clothes and the shaving of his head. This practice of tearing one's clothes referred to the tearing of one's outer garment or mantle. The act physically demonstrated the attempt to remove the anguish felt by the loss.

It is an instruction by the priests referenced in the book of Leviticus (10:6). The Israelites were given permission to let their hair become "loose," and they were allowed to rend their garments as a sign of mourning. This is still practiced today at Jewish funerals in the ritual known as Keriah (Rabinowicz 1994).

That being said, Job's grief is not an affront to God; we know that based on verse 22. Verse 21 holds the words of a true servant of God, going back to what I referred to earlier as a notion of God. When you seek God in the little things, your natural reaction will be to seek God in the big things. Too often, we seek God only when it comes to the big things, and that means our relationship with God is probably not as solid as it could be.

That's what happened to me in the moment of my grief and devastation. I went to a place of *This can't hurt me*. I know where that line of thinking originated from. I blame it on being a child of the eighties, where "real men" didn't show emotion. Job was a real man and served God in all he did. When the hurt came, he knew right where to go. His words in verse 21 are a testimony to the notion of God in his heart and mind.

He understands that he is a steward over all that he is given— including his children. He releases what has been given to him, back to God, from where it came. That last part is where many of us struggle. In pain and heartache, many find it challenging to bless God. I see Job's example as a place we can get to in our relationship with God.

Honoring God's faithfulness and mercy in the depths of our pain is the truest sign of spiritual maturity. When you have arrived at the place in your relationship with God where in the height of your heartache you can praise and worship God, then you know your heart is in the right place. Job was prepared for this and responded in kind. What he wasn't prepared for were the questions that would soon consume him.

Job's pain does not end with heartache; it goes further into physical pain. The Bible tells us that Satan afflicts Job with boils from the crown of his head to the bottom of his feet (Job 2:7). Perhaps the pain from this physical affliction allowed him a moment of emotional relief to divert his focus from the void he felt in his heart. We learn that he scrapes these sores to find relief from the immense pain. The physical pain is not the end of this onslaught. His biggest test is about to present itself from the one place you would least expect it.

During this new level of suffering, Job's wife enters the scene. It is the first and last we will hear from her. "Curse God and die" (Job 2:9). These words seem callous and hard from a woman who could have been the support Job needed to endure this difficult season of his life. You may be thinking of some choice words Job should have snapped back at her. "Why don't you take a long walk off a short pier?" "What broom did you ride in on?" But his response demonstrates the notion in his mind as a servant of God.

> He replied, "You are talking like a foolish woman.
> Shall we accept good from God, and not trouble?"
> (Job 2:10 NIV)

His frustration is apparent. He challenges his wife to consider God's blessings as well as the trials that are delivered from God. He knows there is purpose in the presence of all this pain.

It is true that behind every great man there is a great woman. Whether it be a wife or a mother or even a child, women have the power to make men heroes in their most desperate of moments. But consider what she has lost. She has been subjected to a similar fate as Job. The ten children she carried, nursed, and raised are now gone. Her livelihood is vacant, and now her godly husband chooses to cling to his integrity. She demands that he be realistic and not cling to what she believes to be religious fanaticism.

Women care for their families so that they might ensure the stability of their lives and the lives of others. When stability is jeopardized in the home, there is a helpless feeling that permeates a woman's soul, and her heart begins to tear slowly from one end to another. Job's wife has a broken heart and no longer wants to see her husband suffer. Her response may seem callous, but under the circumstances, I can see why she said what she said.

In moments of suffering, we often turn to family for support and comfort. Often the challenge for our family can be that they have a difficult time understanding our circumstances or being able to identify with our pain. Some will write it off and dismiss what we are attempting to convey as something we need to just get over. Others may enable our bad behavior when we choose pity over integrity.

As we see with Job, family can sometimes interfere with the hope that comes from seeking God in our suffering. This is why it is important to place God first in our lives. It is not Job's wife's responsibility to assuage his suffering. I know many will disagree.

Consider the forces working against Job and his family. This is not something he or she can do in the absence of God. This is an important example for us to remember in the midst of suffering.

Whatever tragedy has struck your life, know that there are forces working in that tragedy that you and I cannot comprehend. Paul made it clear to the Philippians what was possible. Yes, you and I can do all things—but only through Christ and the hope that he offers each of us (Phil. 4:13).

WHY

This is where the substance of the book of Job begins to shine. No one gets through life without asking, "Why?" When my mother took her own life, when I was only nine, I spent years asking God to tell me why. I was so consumed by her passing that my physical development was impacted. I was 5'2" as a sophomore in high school. I was 6'2" as a senior in high school.

There were many other indications of my delayed development that manifested not only physically but mentally and emotionally. I was convinced I could change the past and refused to move forward until I found a way. Asking why is not the issue. Being consumed with the answer is the problem. As my dad used to say, "Don't get attached to the outcome."

We as Christians are encouraged to have a relationship with God. This relationship is rooted in honesty. How successful have you been in hiding things from God?

Being honest with ourselves and honest with those around us leads to healthy and strong relationships. God is no different, except for the fact that he knows your heart before you do. He seeks honesty in your prayers. All too often, we get caught up in the idea that God doesn't need to hear from us, that he knows what's going on. He does know; that's a given.

So here is the interesting element to voicing anything with God. If he already knows yet desires to hear it from us, then who is it really for? It's for us. He wants us to vocalize our pain. Consider the psalms—the joy, pain, happiness, and loss that David conveys. This is pleasing to God's ear. More importantly, it is the beginning of healing and forgiveness for us.

I have encountered so many Christians who believe it's not acceptable to express anger to God—or any other emotion for that matter. Raw, honest, and authentic emotion is what God wants from your heart. When you lay your emotions before God, when you strip your heart bare before your Savior, you have demonstrated your willingness to surrender that hurt to the only one who can release you from it. This is another characteristic of servants of God. The next time you are suffering, the next time the weight of tragedy overwhelms your heart, take a moment, get on your knees and place the pieces of your broken heart before God and watch him begin to heal your life.

Job is not left alone to seek answers for his suffering. He is visited by several friends that begin to challenge the limitations of his "uprightness." Bildad, Eliphaz, and Zophar come to Job in the time of his suffering. Friends are often present when they are aware of our suffering. They come to console us, to empathize with us, and to be present as we endure our pain. Job's friends provide part of that formula.

Somehow, the empathy runs short with these three as they begin to judge, criticize, accuse, and undermine Job in this difficult time. Some of the best humor comes from these chapters as Job responds to their thoughtless responses with sarcasm and disdain. "You are all worthless physicians" (Job 13:4) and "Miserable comforters are you all!" (Job 16:2) are just a few of the responses Job musters in his pain. Many find him to be impatient and rude, but keep in mind that suffering tends to wear our patience thin.

These events affect our self-esteem, especially when it comes to illness. Job expresses this blow to his self-esteem: "Even if I am righteous I cannot lift up my head. I am full of disgrace; See my misery!" (Job 10:15). Suffering and tragedy affect us on every level, spiritually, mentally, and even molecularly. The changes our entire being undergoes during these times is a testament to the creation that is the human body. It is also an indication of the reliance we have on a creator.

Consider the last tragedy you endured. Acknowledge the stages you went through and the healing you experienced in every aspect of your being. Reflect on the friends and family present at that time. I would venture that many were understanding and empathetic, while others said the wrong thing at the wrong time. Many of them are not capable and may never understand what you went through. The takeaway is to remember that not all our friends make the best counselors.

Job's suffering is severe, and his confusion regarding his circumstances consumes him. He has spent his life serving God and keeping his commandments. He, an upright and just man, now finds himself as ground zero for this chaos, pain, and loss. Job spends the time he has with his friends presenting his case of being blameless. He demands to reason with God (Job 13:3). It is not unnatural for him to want an audience with his accuser. At one point, he identifies what must be the answer to all that has befallen him. "God has delivered me to the ungodly" (Job 16:11).

As he exhausts all possibilities of the reasons behind these events, he turns to the most obvious explanation, that God has handed him over to the wicked. His friends offer little assistance in understanding. They berate him with evidence of the wicked being punished, implying that Job is wicked.

Their explanations are riddled with an empty and hollow understanding of God's design surrounding tragedy. All that they offer job is the antithesis of wise counsel in this moment. I believe this only fuels the fire of Job's frustration. Remember that prayer turns our tragedy into purpose. It is important to emphasize our vertical conversation during our suffering. Too often, it is God attempting to get our attention.

Whether it be to challenge us to see his design and purpose or to identify an area we have yet to surrender in our lives, the reasons behind God allowing suffering and tragedy are not important. Our response is what matters in the end.

SACRIFICE

If you have not read God's response to Job in chapters 38 through 41, I encourage you to do so. It is a humbling and elegant response that provides us an understanding of God's power, glory, and sovereignty.

As I studied for this chapter, I got caught up in the poetry of the book of Job, as if I were back in college being mystified by Shakespeare. I kept being brought back to the beginning. Before the tragedy, before the suffering, to the moment when God looks at Job and says, "Have you considered my servant Job …".

I cannot imagine the depth of Job's grief or the grief of anyone who loses a child. As I sat back, a question entered my mind. *Why did God allow Satan to take those ten beautiful, vibrant children?* I realized quickly that I was seeing these events unfold linearly. We often see cause and effect as it relates to us and our world. As I mentioned earlier, consider seeing the end at the beginning of your decisions.

Imagine you saw the whole world all at once. You were right now able to see the relationships between action and reaction. Now take a moment. What if you saw it all from the beginning of time to the end of time? God begins this book with a challenge from Satan, and the ultimate lesson is about God responding to Satan's challenge.

Yes, God used Job to provide a dramatic medium for a response to Satan, but consider how this story ends. His response to Job is sufficient; he restores Job and his family. The book of Job is filled with beautiful imagery and poetic verse, all of which is valuable to our daily lives, but the overarching theme of Job is the story between God and Satan.

God knew the end at the beginning. He knew all that would happen to Job, every decision he would make. The outcome was not just about restoring Job; it was so much larger than that. We are engaged in this very discourse because of what God allowed to happen to Job. Sure, he saw the suffering and tragedy that Job and his wife would endure, but he also saw the moment he would reveal his nature to Job, the values and lessons that would come out of the exchange between Bildad, Eliphaz, Zophar, and Job. Ultimately, he saw the value that is the book of Job for future generations and how Job's example would allow us to learn more about who God is and his purpose for our pain.

Key Reflections

Take time to consider some of the key points of Job's life and his tragedy:

- Consider a tragedy you have faced or are currently facing. What purpose do you think God has for it?

- How can you take the example Job's friends provided in his suffering and apply it to your friends going through tragedy?

- How can you respond to the suffering of your spouse in a way that honors God?

- Is there a way to have a better understanding of the outcome of the decisions you make?

- How have the tragedies of your past shaped who you are today?

- When tragedy strikes, how will you make God a part of those moments?

Chapter 4
LEADER

I SHOWED UP EARLY to get my bearings. It was my first semester of college and even more importantly my first day of PT at ROTC. I felt rather out of place with my ROTC running shorts and my T-Shirt with "Air force ROTC" written boldly across the front in white letters. I looked more like an advertisement than a hard-charging cadet. The one advantage to wearing such an outfit was it wasn't hard to know who to follow. I quickly saw a gaggle of other similarly dressed people standing together, and I quickly approached them to somehow feel as if I had found where I belonged.

The truth was I knew no one there and I was feeling extremely out of place. "Attention!" I heard a senior cadet yell as the commandant walked out of the building and toward our group. I immediately struck the pose, attempting to work my best Pete Mitchell impersonation from *Top Gun*.

We were quickly divided into our squads for PT and ushered off on a two-mile run through the streets of Tempe, Arizona. I remember listening to the senior cadets call cadence and order us into formation as we ran. It was fascinating to see groups of thirty cadets running in unison, and being a part of it was even more impressive.

PT led to parade drills on the field. I remember getting my lefts and rights correct. I remember doing well in the march off, a drill that was somewhat of a last man standing of following marching orders. Senior cadets were typically the ones calling the commands as we marched around the field.

One day, I was called front and center to one of the cadet commanders. I reported as requested and was informed I would be leading the cadets in parade drills that day. The world started to become dark, my hearing started to fail, and my breathing became shallow.

All of these days of drilling, and I had never paid much attention to how to lead a group. I quickly took my place at the edge of the field and called "Attention!" I panicked. I couldn't remember a single command. The troop stood there and waited for my order. "Forward march!" I quickly shouted. The group began to move. "Left, left, your left, right, left!" I called out a cadence as a way of hiding my panic. I couldn't for the life of me remember the other commands.

As I continued to call out cadence, I noticed the group had stopped. "As you were, sir!" a cadet called out from the group. My attention went back to the group, and I realized they were all marching in place.

As I looked in horror, I realized the problem. I had marched them directly into a wall. "Ready, halt!" a senior cadet called out. "About-face!" another command. "Cadet Middagh! Return to formation!" I promptly saluted and went back to my place in the formation. I was never asked to lead parade drills again. That probably had more to do with me dropping out of college than my performance that day.

Being a leader is one of the greatest challenges anyone of us will face. Leadership takes on so many different forms through many venues. There are enough books on leadership to fill a thousand libraries. One of those books would undoubtedly be the Bible.

Being called to lead is not always glamourous and often does not come with an appropriate title. A call to lead may show up, as it did for me, on a day you least expect it. If we break it down and are honest with ourselves, we lead a lot more often than we realize.

Consider what it takes to be a leader as a parent. You may not think the trips to soccer practice and PTA meetings are activities of a leader, but they are. In the book of Hebrews, the author shares, "Remember your leaders, who spoke the word of God to you. Consider the outcome of their way of life and imitate their faith" (Hebrews 13:7).

Any leadership book will tell you that leadership is about action and setting an example in that action. As a parent, you are asked to lead every day. Children learn through observation, and when we as parents choose to show up and act on their behalf, it may not seem like it, but that's the epitome of leadership.

FORGED

How does God forge us into leaders for his purpose? God calls on leaders are called on by God to make a difference. In some cases, they are big differences, like altering the course of history. In other instances, they are small ways that change the lives of just one or two people. Leaders are, I know its cliché but, crafted through trial by fire.

Remember your first child, or your first time driving a car, or the first promotion where people reported to you. These moments are filled with fear, and in many cases, they are presented as obligations in the lives we lead. In other words, once we are in them, there's no turning back. As a result, we are forced to face our fears and charge forward.

Now compare your second child, driving a car now, or that leadership role you have held at the company for ten years. Not as scary as the first time. What separates the parent you were when your firstborn entered the world from the parent you are now? Experience, hardship, and adversity have led you to having confidence in your ability.

It took those sleepless nights and moments of terror to forge you into the parent you are today. God carves leaders out of experience, hardship, and trials. Why is this his recipe for forging the leader key? Consider what James has to offer regarding trials:

> Consider it pure joy, my brothers and sisters, whenever you face trials of many kinds, because you know that the testing of your faith produces perseverance. Let perseverance finish its work so that you may be mature and complete, not lacking anything. (James 1:2–4 NIV)

In these verses, James emphasizes the significance of trials in our lives and the role they play. More importantly, he outlines what our response should be. God's motives for using adversity to shape us has more to do with how we are wired than how he operates. Some of us are overconfident and independent. Others are fearful creatures by nature, they are self-doubting, and self-deprecating.

I suspect doubt is what drove Adam and Eve to hit the drive-through at the one joint in Eden they were told not to. When called to a leadership role, we default to lacking confidence. God understands this and challenges us to rely on him first. The beauty in this is to reflect on your first child, your first driving exam, and your first leadership role and remember it differently.

What if the first time you heard your child cry, you knew beyond a shadow of a doubt you were not alone? What if when that first police car pulled up behind you while driving toward that intersection, you were in a high-occupancy vehicle? What if during that first meeting with your new team of employees, you had a confidant cheering you on? God wants you to remember that you are never alone, and he wants you to seek him when fear is all you see.

Consider the outcome had Adam and Eve talked to God before making that history-altering decision. We see examples of this even in Jesus's ministry. In the fourteenth chapter of Matthew, Peter challenges Jesus to an identity contest.

A man walks on water, and another man walks on water. That's enough to keep your audience interested. What I find more intriguing is that it was Peter's idea. "Lord if it's you," Peter replied, "tell me to come to you on the water" (Matthew 12:28). I want to make sure I understand this. Two seconds prior, you thought this man was a ghost. You are obviously still unsure who it is, and now you are ready to jump ship and see if water walking is your new X Games sport?

Jesus responds with one word: "Come." Always the boastful one Peter. Always with something to prove. I like that about Peter; he's a doer. He's ready to try this whole water-walking bit, and sure enough, he pulls it off like a champ—well, up to a point. As we all know, Peter begins to sink. What changed? What caused Peter to go from champion water walker to drowned disciple? He took his eyes off the prize.

This passage is filled with so much of what leadership in life is all about. First Peter takes it upon himself to be the one to take the risk, establishing himself as a leader. Jesus calls him out. This is very important; always remember when going before God with a challenge to be prepared for his answer. Peter, not wanting to be seen as fearful, takes the initiative; after all, his friends are watching.

His act of faith, in and of itself is what places his feet firmly upon those uneasy waters. What is even more interesting is we know for a fact that Jesus is the conductor of this symphony of waves. We have seen him calm the storms and the waves in other events in the Bible. He could have made this watery crescendo into a quiet, shallow ballad for Peter if he wanted to. If he were to do that, it wouldn't be capitalizing on this character-building moment for Peter, now would it?

Jesus doesn't calm the storm for Peter; no, he lets Peter focus on the chaos around him. Upon losing sight of the author and finisher of his faith, he begins to sink. Despite this lapse in faith, Jesus rescues him from the water. This is a leadership lesson.

As leaders, we all get in over our heads. We all begin to rely on our strength and understanding. In that moment is when we begin to sink, where previously we had solid footing.

Remember Peter when this happens, and remember he cried out to Jesus. When the waves seem larger than your faith, don't lose sight of what's really going on. Those waves are just Jesus letting you know you don't have to do this alone.

GRACEFUL

The examples of men and women becoming leaders for God in the Bible are rarely graceful. Many of them become leaders through no uncertain circumstances. Consider Esther, David, and Moses. All of these people found themselves in leadership roles in God's organizational chart by a series of events that none of them would have expected. I can imagine a modern-day interview with David.

"So, David, our readers are asking, what's it like being the leader of the nation of God?"

"Well, with a boss like mine, it's rewarding, and at the same time, there is a lot to live up to."

"Tell me, did you see yourself here, now, with all this responsibility?"

"If someone had told me that picking a fight with a Philistine giant would land me here, I would have told them they were crazy."

God often sets the stage and the path for us to enter our leadership role without even knowing what's going on. We will come back to David in another chapter, but for now, I want to focus on another figure that has permeated our history and our culture—a man named Moses.

The majority of the world could identify Moses without much effort. Born into a Levite family, saved by a Pharaoh's daughter, he was raised in luxury only to be ostracized from his home. He was confronted by God and returned to the scene of the crime only to spend years wandering in the desert with God's chosen people.

I do not believe humanity is creative enough to fabricate this story. It is filled with aspects of the human condition and our natural tendencies when it comes to encountering God. When you begin to consider documentaries such as *Patterns in Exodus* and *Exodus Decoded*, you come face-to-face with the Moses experience. These films provide background and evidence for the biblical story of the Exodus. For those who consider Moses to be a fictitious character of mythology and legend, I encourage spending an afternoon with these two great documentaries. It may just change your life.

The background we are provided about Moses is rather detailed. Born in a time when the Israelites were enslaved to the Egyptian empire. Add to this the maniacal ravings of a lunatic Pharaoh, and you have a recipe for the most threatening world a Hebrew baby boy could be born into.

Given a death sentence at birth by the Pharaoh, Moses's mother sees him as healthy and beautiful and fears for his safety. She decided, despite the potential consequences, to hide him for three months.

It is not uncommon for my study of the Bible to be met with the desire for more information. Being analytical, I constantly ask questions and, in this case, a whole host of questions come to mind. *What was Moses's father thinking about this plan? How in the world do you hide an infant for three months in their circumstances? What did she name this little boy?*

That last one stands out for me. The text never identifies his name. The name Moses was given to him by the Pharaoh's daughter. Did his real mother convince Pharaoh's daughter to give him that name? Perhaps her fear of losing him prevented her from naming him.

The answers I typically find in these situations is that none of those questions matter because God is in control. Moses's mother eventually saw that raising this young boy was going to be too difficult to do in secret. She took a risk and placed him in a basket and sent him down the river. There is nothing to indicate that she knew what would happen to Moses. His sister, Mariam, is the one who keeps an eye on him as he travels down this river of opportunity.

VULNERABLE

God intervenes in some of our most vulnerable moments. At this point, Moses is at his most vulnerable. He is three months old in a basket floating down a river. Despite being this vulnerable, he is not alone. God ensures his next encounter will be the one to set a plan and purpose in motion that change Israel's history forever. The

Pharaoh's daughter finds this basket, decides to adopt this young boy, and names him Moses. Moses enters the palace and is raised by his own mother. This is significant. He is raised by his Levite mother for twelve years and is taught the customs and history of his heritage.

One of the common patterns we encounter in the Bible is that, often, the people God calls are dual citizens. We will begin to touch on this more and more throughout this book. Moses is no different; he is duplicitous in his association. He is a Levite first but an Egyptian as well. Raised with the understanding of both customs and cultures, he is a liaison between the two nations. Possessing this dual citizenship provides him with a unique perspective as well as a comprehensive skill set that will pay dividends in the future.

Moses will not truly understand his purpose for another seventy years. His entrance into this world is nothing glamorous. His childhood and adolescence are filled with confusion and questions. God allows our free will and the free will of others to present less than ideal circumstances. He is sovereign, but he is not a dictator.

Moses does not immediately see the plight of the Israelites. It's not until he is older that he realizes their situation and at one point takes drastic measures to intervene. Throughout Moses's life, we see a leader being born. Not just a leader but—a leader for a specific purpose. Consider for a moment the tragedies that befell Moses and his family—almost murdered at birth, taken from his home, eventually estranged from all that he has known. This is all in the first forty years of his life.

STEWARD

As a parent, it is often difficult to understand the tragedies our children endure. We often take responsibility for their suffering. We somehow see ourselves as being in control of not just their lives but all that they may encounter. When a tragedy occurs, we think, *I should have protected them from that.* God doesn't want your purpose to be empty or insignificant.

Regardless of whether you are a parent or the leader of a Fortune 500 company, he wants your life to have meaning, your character to have substance, and your understanding to have wisdom.

Meaning, substance and wisdom come from enduring life's challenges. Without Moses's upbringing and tragedy, he would never have been able to succeed as God's chosen leader for his people. I cannot imagine what it must take to send your son down a river in a basket, but I can guarantee it takes faith.

It also takes a mental shift from what our culture would lead us to believe. That mental shift is that our children do not belong to us. Just as we are called to be stewards of everything we are given, we are also called to be stewards of our children. Tomorrow is not guaranteed, for us or our children. Moses's mother knew this and placed her faith and trust along with her son in a basket and released him to God's purpose for his life.

Few of us will make it through this life without regrets. Typically, those regrets are surrounded by guilt and shame. It could be we hurt someone we love, or we hurt ourselves. Perhaps it's an event that cost you a relationship or a career opportunity. Most regrets are rooted in reflecting on what could have been.

One absolute about regrets is that the circumstances that led up to the event were orchestrated by us and our own will. God doesn't do regret, and his plan for your life will never leave you with regrets. That being said, any regrets you do have I can promise you were decisions you made without seeking his counsel first. Moses had just such an event, coming to the aid of an abused Hebrew and murdering his oppressor in the process. If we were part of a jury panel, many of us would issue a "not guilty" verdict in *The People v. Moses.*

Killing an abusive Egyptian to save the life of another man seems open and shut. From a legal perspective, the defense of a third party is a plausible position to take in a trial. We may see it this way, but someone didn't, and that someone was another Israelite.

Some interesting details come out of this encounter as it is depicted in the Bible. Moses looks around to be sure there are no witnesses and then kills the Egyptian and hides his body in the sand (Exodus 2:12). This makes sense. Moses knew that regardless of the circumstances, killing an Egyptian over a Hebrew meant a death sentence for him.

In this instance, he relies upon his own strength and understanding. Many of us would intervene when seeing a similar situation unfold. The act of defending his fellow Hebrew is not the problem. It's the degree to which he defended this man and the hiding of the body that illuminates Moses's lack of faith.

Moses is forty years old by now, and people know him as the Pharaoh's grandson. I am no expert, but I am sure he could have intervened without killing this Egyptian. Even if that wasn't the case, he could have remembered that just as God was in control when Moses was placed in that basket and sent down the river, God was in control now.

Moses's fear got the best of him, and he hid the body so no one would find out. Someone did find out, but I have a feeling that everyone knew what Moses had done, at least within the Hebrew community.

We don't know much about this victim, but let's call him Simon. Now Simon is beaten by this Egyptian, and the Pharaoh's grandson intervenes and saves his life. If I'm Simon, I am telling everyone I know why I am alive. Too often, when we deny the truth about ourselves and what we've done, reality comes knocking on our door to collect, and when that happens, running seems to be the most obvious solution.

HAPPILY EVER AFTER

Our mistakes, regardless of how trivial or brutal they are, are never far from us as people. For some of us, they haunt us daily to the point we can barely function. They destroy our self-esteem, confiscate our hope, and leave us desperate. Others bury them, deny them, drink them, or rationalize them into oblivion. Regardless, they never quite depart from us.

Moses knew that what he was about to do would have consequences, and thousands of years later, it's easy for me to sit here and pick apart his decisions. The purpose of this is to identify our nature when it comes to injustice. We get angry when we see injustice.

It's our default, as empathetic creatures, to want justice for the victimized. One thing I can promise you is no amount of anger, retaliation, or empathy comes close to the way God sees injustice. God makes do with our mistakes. He allows us to act of our own understanding, and it can cost us and those around us dearly. The peace we lack as a result of our mistakes is not God's doing; it's ours. He is always ready and willing to forgive and to heal your life so that you can become the key to unlocking your true purpose in his plan.

What do you do when you have murdered someone and the consequences are death? No trial, no jury—just death. Well, you relocate. Sunny, beautiful, exotic Midian. What's interesting is not that Moses runs but where he ends up. When we run from our mistakes, we often don't plan where we are going to end up very well. It's more about getting away from something than getting to something.

God is still working in Moses's life even during this chaos and tragedy. He is using Moses's mistakes to forge him into the leader he will one day need to be. So, does the running away work? Well, for a period, yes. Moses gets married, finds a career he is good at, and has a family. All is well. I am sure the story could have ended here—man flees from his accusers for a justified crime and gets a second chance. Sounds like the plot to a movie. New life, new family, new home. Why do we need to go any further than that" I feel a "and they lived happily ever after" coming on.

COMPLACENCY

In our moments of complacency, God has a tendency to confront us with our past. Leaders are often forced to consider their past. The best leaders are those who reflect on where they have been and acknowledge not just their failures but also their successes. God, in confronting Moses, challenges him to leave his life, his family, and his responsibilities, to go on what appears to be a suicide mission.

Consider, right now, as you are reading this book, a bush in your front yard lit on fire. God reveals himself to you and asks you right now to drop everything in your life and go deal with your past and at the same time save an entire nation. I don't know about you, but I am quite comfortable with my cup of coffee and my office chair. Moses could have easily taken the same approach. Instead, when confronted with God, he is humbled.

> "Who am I that I should go to Pharaoh, and that I should bring the children of Israel out of Egypt?" (Exodus 3:11 NKJV)

Notice God's response.

> "I will certainly be with you. And this shall be a sign to you that I have sent you: When you have brought

the people out of Egypt, you shall serve God on this mountain." (Exodus 3:12 NKJV)

Moses has it straight from the burning bush that he is not alone. He is being called to lead, and he is not alone. This is easy to read but difficult to apply. When God calls you to lead, He will never ask you to do it alone. The other element in God's response the outline of his plan. Notice how despite the obstacle in front of Moses, God is absolute about what will happen. He doesn't say "if" you bring them out of Egypt, he says "when."

God is jumping to the end of the book before Moses has even embraced the gravity of his new circumstances. What I love about this is the conviction. God is giving Moses an example of the conviction he will need to carry out this task. *Moses, you will do this so that you can serve me on this mountain.* God is so interested in getting to the Moses-serving-him part that he almost glosses over the daunting task of extricating the Israelites from their oppressors. Keep in mind the Israelites were an integral part of the Egyptian economic model.

Free labor has been the foundation of many an economic system throughout history, and whenever it is threatened, wars usually transpire. Moses is not concerned with that. His concern is about the Israelites. Moses wants to know, "Whom shall I say is calling?" God lays out his plan to Moses in detail. Nothing is left out. This was for Moses's benefit and for God's glory.

Moses is making a good effort in trying to think of everything before he goes on this little errand for God. *What if they don't believe me? I'm not a good orator. I don't want to do this alone.* This is the humanity of Moses. This is the stuff that allows you and I to relate to Moses. We would feel the same way.

Doubt is the biggest enemy of a leader. God wants to extinguish all doubt for Moses, and he provides him with the means to extinguish not only his own doubts but the doubts of those who will soon follow him. Moses lacks confidence at this point; it is not until he sees the signs and wonders from God that he overcomes his fear and sets out to take part in fulfilling his purpose in God's plan.

Reluctant leaders like Moses often don't realize the value of their skills. Did Moses need all these things to accomplish God's commands? The answer is no. God's commands will be fulfilled regardless of what we need to overcome our self-doubt. The wonder and beauty of God is his ability and desire to meet us where we are at the height of our doubt and fear.

Confident leaders typically end up on the other side of the track. "I can do it by myself." "I don't need any help." The danger here is when we are leading under our own confidence, we tend to hurt those around us without even realizing it. Regardless of where you are in your leadership role, remember to always involve God. He is interested in you and your plight and the difficulties you face. He wants to be involved but only if you invite him to do so.

OCTOGENARIAN

Moses is finally confronted with his purpose in God's plan eighty years into his life. Why eighty years? God's plans don't always consult your calendar or your desire for when, where, and how you want to fulfill God's purpose. For Moses, I'm sure he was content to live out his days as a shepherd for Jethro's flocks. He had eighty years of tragedy and training to become one of the greatest leaders in history.

Being raised both Hebrew and Egyptian, his dual citizenship will eventually provide him the means to be an advocate for the Israelites to the Egyptians. His standing with the Egyptian leadership provides him a unique position to speak to Pharaoh and enter his court. All the years of being a shepherd teach him about life in the wilderness and the necessary patience to lead God's people for forty years.

His whole life was one incident after another that eventually led him to his ultimate purpose, setting God's people free. In the absence of all his tragedy, the story of Moses may have ended the day he was born.

Key Reflections

Take time to consider some of the key points of Moses's life and his leadership:

- How has tragedy from your childhood shaped you as an adult?

- In which areas of your life are you a leader?

- Whom do you set an example for?

- What mistakes have you buried or run from?

- How has God challenged you to face those mistakes?

- Who or what does God put in your life to help you overcome your doubts?

- As a leader, what areas of your life will you invite God to be a part of?

Chapter 5

CHARACTER

I WAS NEVER A soldier. I never felt the sting of adrenaline race through my veins as battle approached. I was never a king. My head has never carried the heavy weight of a crown. As is apparent, I was never a poet. My words have never been filled with rhythm or rhyme. I've never been hunted. No king has ever

> Nearly all men can stand adversity, but if you want to test a man's character, give him power.
>
> —Abraham Lincoln

placed a bounty upon my head. Nor have I ever encountered an armor-clad giant bent on wiping my name from history. As I write these achievements down, I think about what it would take to become or endure any one of them. What if your résumé contained these skill sets? What kind of person would you have to be to take on this much responsibility? Each one of these professions demands a level of commitment and discipline that is easily admired but virtually impossible to carry out with composure and integrity. I see within each of them a common element—character.

As a soldier, you are asked to place your life in harm's way in the service of others. Knowing you could perish at the hand of a stranger, for a stranger, and doing so despite the outcome takes character. Becoming a king or queen while never knowing the burden you will have to carry, yet accepting the responsibility anyway, requires character. The art of poetry demands a level of understanding around emotion and the human condition. Poetry is writing about character or lack thereof.

King David and I have little in common. David's story reads like a script from a Ridley Scott film. So much of the challenge that David faced shaped him to becoming the greatest king of the Old Testament, a king that still revered today by the nation of Israel. Jerusalem, to this day, is known as the City of David. The star on the Israeli flag is the star of David. You may be in the same position as I am, not having experienced what David went through. Or maybe you have encountered these situations. David is not without his mistakes. There is one in particular he is most known for—Bathsheba.

Recently, a friend mentioned that David is most known for two events in his life, the day he slew Goliath and the day he encountered Bathsheba. From the time we are small, we are told stories about David and Goliath. I remember watching my Sunday school teacher as she moved a cutout of David across a felt board toward a massive cutout of Goliath.

As children, we are spared from David's catastrophic failure that he experienced later in life. Later, we hear this story for the first time. In my experience, there was an enormous gap. When I first heard about David's encounter with Bathsheba, I kept thinking, *Oh, nothing to worry about this is David. He's got this. He'll do the right thing.* That was not the case. One mistake led to another, which led to another, each progressively getting worse.

Affairs, lies, murder—this must be some other David in the Bible. How many Johns, James, and Simons are there in the Bible? This must be some other David. My childhood hero had been tarnished. He was no longer what I wanted to be when I grew up. My experience with David's indiscretion was similar to the experience others had.

We hear about his victory against Goliath and then hear about his downfall with Bathsheba. Somewhere deep inside, we begin to wonder if we are susceptible to such a great fall as David's. The important question is, How did he get from celebrated champion to adulteress murderer?

David's story may be filled with adventure and suspense, but it's not that different from yours and mine. David had numerous giants outside of Goliath to defeat. If you take time to read Malcolm Gladwell's book *David and Goliath,* you will see that Goliath was likely the smallest giant he ever had to defeat. So, what if we emphasize David's other giants and see how he ended up with the wrong woman in his bedroom?

YOUNGEST

I remember hearing stories from my father about life on the farm when he was little. Drinking well water, sleeping in the barn, and using an outhouse, it was a far stretch from my childhood that was filled with indoor plumbing and the earliest of personal computers.

Permeating the backdrop of all the differences between my dad's childhood and mine is an area that all children can relate to. The world is filled with wonder. There is magic in every day and miracles in every moment. As we get older, we lose much of this amazement.

Somehow, magic doesn't show up in our mortgage payment regardless of how much we wish it would. Our childhood is our first introduction to God's glory. As we are brought into this world that he created for us, we are overwhelmed with sights, smells, and sounds. Each of these attaches itself to a memory in our minds. We begin to learn about this place we have been brought into and all the beauty and wonder it has to offer.

David was no different. Sure, he may have not have had access to indoor plumbing or personal computers, but his childhood was filled with wonder. We know he was a shepherd. We know he defeated lions and bears (1 Samuel 17:36). There is, however, another important aspect about David that is often overlooked: he was the youngest of eight sons (1 Samuel 16:6–13).

There is much research surrounding order of birth. In Dr. Kevin Lehman's book, *The Birth Order Book*, he outlines the various intricacies that play a part in how birth order can and does affect everything from your career choices to your personality. What does the research say about being the youngest? They are charming, affectionate, immature, more agreeable, rebellious, empathetic, artistic, persistent, popular, social, confident, attention-loving, impatient, and manipulative (Eckstein et al. 2010)

In looking at that list, I can own quite a few of those, and it makes sense considering I am the youngest in my family. What if we took what we know about David and started applying some of those traits to him. Charismatic, empathetic, artistic, persistent, popular, social, and confident all seem to coincide with the biblical account of David. Charismatic seems appropriate. He convinced Saul to let him fight Goliath. Considering how young he was at the time, this request must have been executed with quite the delivery.

Artistic stands out for obvious reasons. How many instruments did David play? How many did he invent? Spend a month reading Psalms and you will begin to scratch the surface of just how artistic David was. Let's not forget about persistent. I think relentless is a more appropriate depiction. What about the less flattering traits in the list? Immature, rebellious, impatient, and manipulative. That last one stands out: manipulative.

Manipulative—just saying it, the stigma drips from each vowel and consonant. Is manipulation bad? I'm sure many would say, "Absolutely!" I am challenged to look a little deeper. I think David manipulated much of his circumstances throughout his life. When David faced Goliath, he knew he had the upper hand. Highly trained long-distance fighter against lumbering giant? I'd take those odds any day. What about the story of the hundred foreskins (1 Samuel 18:25)?

I imagine this was Saul's way of trying to humiliate David. Any man asks me to go retrieve a hundred foreskins, and I'm going to ask him if he's feeling okay, encourage him to seek some therapy. Not David. He brings back not one hundred but two hundred. When you one-up someone's challenge, you are manipulating your circumstances. Let's not forget about the bathroom incident.

For you men, consider the scene. You're standing in the urinal, the bathroom's empty, it's quiet, and you begin to whistle. You read the latest cave dwellers' news bulletin posted in front of you, finish up your business, walk outside, and realize someone cut your robe while you were handling your business. Not only that, but you realize it only because some yahoo comes running after you, screaming, "Hey, look what I cut off of your robe!" Disturbing, right? I bring these instances up because, where there may be manipulation, it is not necessarily manipulation in the evil sense. No, that happens later.

So, David's the youngest, and it's evident he possesses many characteristics that the youngest are prone to have. What events happen in his youth that begin to shape him into the key God needs him to be to lead Israel? Well, let's start with his anointing.

ANOINTED

Being the youngest is difficult. Everyone else gets the firsts before you do. I was the last born in my immediate family of my sister and I. I was also the youngest of four grandkids. I remember being left out of a lot. I was too little, too young, or just too far apart in age to participate. My older cousins and sister got to experience everything first. First dance, first grade, and first kiss all came for them before it ever arrived at my door.

In hindsight, it was a lot like somebody telling you the plot and the ending of a movie without you ever going to see it. Finally, when you did get to go see it, it wasn't that big a deal to anyone else, and it wasn't that big a deal to you.

I remember calling my older cousin to tell him I got my driver's license. Not really a big deal considering he was on his third car already and had been driving for four years. So being last in the birth order is accompanied by perpetual disappointments; however, this is not to say that the youngest don't sometimes find ways to shine on their own.

I had a friend Mark who was a police officer. He was the youngest in his family and always felt the need to prove himself. It didn't help that he was shorter than his brothers. I remember hearing him tell a story about a thanksgiving dinner one year. His older brother, Tony the lawyer, showed up and began to recite his accoutrements as if reading them from a receipt. "Rolex, five Gs; Armani suit, three Gs, shoes, eight hundred; tie; three hundred; BMW, eighty-five thousand."

Tony shared each item at the table with a smile on his face, a proud grin as he rattled off the cost of each of his trophies. Mark sat quietly at the table in his uniform and ate as his brother recited these items. Tony turned to him and said, "When are you going to arrive at greatness, little brother?"

Mark wiped his mouth, took a drink, and quietly responded, "Ballistic vest, one G; duty belt and equipment, two Gs; patrol car, $115,000; hundreds of lives saved … priceless."

In hearing this story, I quickly recognized the desperate need that the youngest often have to prove themselves not only to their siblings but to their family as a whole. Some of that comes from just being the youngest. All too often, the issues associated with being the youngest are exacerbated by what older siblings do to lean on the pain points of the youngest.

David was no exception. Being the youngest of eight boys, I'm sure he always felt he had something to prove. We witness this treatment even in his anointing. His father doesn't even consider him as an option. Even Samuel had preconceived notions about what the next king would look like.

What we see here is God's election by the state of a person's heart, not by their appearance (1 Samuel 16:7). He was chosen to be last by his family but chosen to be first by God. I hear an echo of Jesus in this moment of David's anointing. *Whoever is first will be last, and whoever is last will be first.* What does this anointing do for David in his family? It is the one thing that allows him to shine in the shadow of his brothers. We see a glimpse of how he may have used this anointing to his advantage.

In the biblical account of the encounter David has with Goliath, we hear David's older brother comment on David's intention for being there.

> When Eliab, David's oldest brother, heard him speaking with the men, he burned with anger at him and asked, "Why have you come down here?

And with whom did you leave those few sheep in the wilderness? I know how conceited you are and how wicked your heart is; you came down only to watch the battle." (1 Samuel 17:28 NIV)

Eliab challenges David's intention as to why he is at the battlefield. In the same conversation, he attempts to humiliate him by commenting on the "few sheep" he is responsible for. He sees his brother as conceited. These reveal to us the nature of the relationship David had with his older brother. Something interesting is buried in this verse. Notice what Eliab says about David's heart. It's wicked.

So now we have two perspectives. David is a man after God's own heart, and because of his heart, God chooses him to be the next king. Despite this, his brother accuses him of having a wicked heart. What is it about David that causes Eliab to see him as wicked but God to see him as worthy of leadership?

David was not shy about advertising being anointed by God's prophet, instead of his brothers. I think it was the one thing he had to rub in their faces when they teased him. Being chosen by God does something to a person. It can make you fearless. It can make you confident.

The question I ask is, What did being overlooked by God do to Eliab? If only we had an example of someone who might have been chosen as king, someone who was in line to be king and gets overlooked for David. Maybe if we had that person, we could understand the appropriate response to being overlooked.

Saul was king, and as king, it only makes sense that his son would inherit the throne. We gain a detailed profile of Saul's son, Jonathan, through the book of Samuel. His devotion and dedication to David is unprecedented. It could be argued that Jonathan's devotion to

David is not even seen in the devotion the disciples have to Jesus during his ministry.

Jonathan is not even considered by God for the throne, and Saul sees David's success and popularity forfeiting Jonathan's succession. Saul goes as far as to curse Jonathan and his mother because of Jonathan's devotion to David (1 Samuel 20:30). What Jonathan saw in David is the hope for the future of Israel.

He knew his father wasn't capable of ensuring their success or prosperity, and in his heart, he knew because of his father's failings he would never be king. This is an example of getting out of your own way to embrace God's plan for someone else. Jonathan is critical to the success of David becoming king. He assists David in his escape from Saul and even acts as a liaison between his father and David (1 Samuel 19:4–7).

Sometimes God calls us to support and encourage those he has called for a greater purpose. This doesn't trivialize our significance or role in God's plan. Sometimes God calls us to be the key to unlock his purpose in someone else's life.

Consider for a moment being Billy Graham, a world-renowned pastor who has led millions to Christ through his ministry and teaching. Author, speaker, teacher who has influenced world policy. Had his picture taken with leaders from all over the world. Quite the purpose to behold. Hard to imagine being Billy Graham. Now imagine being the person who led Billy Graham to Christ. Each of us has a role to play in God's plan. Some are more visible than others, but I promise you none are trivial.

BORED

"It's good to be the king." My dad always used to say that. As I recall, it was a reference to a Mel Brooks movie, *History of the World—Part*

I. Being king, however, is not easy. Diplomacy, politics, budgets, war, and managing family matters in the midst of it all makes for a constant battle to maintain one's sanity. David was a warrior for much of his adolescence. He fought lions and bears, giants, armies, and even kings. He was undefeated.

I remember reading once that if a game is too easy, you will mess it up just to make it more interesting. This is why video games have difficulty settings. It's what causes some people to sabotage relationships. It all comes back to being bored. You may ask, How can a king be bored? Kings are busy, right? Boredom has little to do with being busy. Many of us would agree that the repetitive days we endure, day in and day out, are filled with activities, but the degree of challenge in those activities is low.

At one time, driving was an adventure and challenging. But after years of driving in traffic and at speeds of up to 75 mph, we often find ourselves arriving at our destination without even knowing how we got there. David's life had prepared him for adventure, for intrigue. It had not prepared him for being bored.

In 2 Samuel 11, we are told that David sent his army off to fight the Ammonites, and he stayed behind. Why stay behind? David's army had a multitude of success, and he considered himself undefeated. For a warrior, this takes the fun out of going to war.

When all you ever do is win, it makes the game predictable. He had confidence in his men, in his generals, and most importantly in God. He had witnessed firsthand God's faithfulness. So, this spring, he decides to stay home. First mistake. When you have the heart of a warrior, go be a warrior, especially when you are given that profession by the God of the universe. It's what I call staying in your lane.

God imprints his purpose for our lives on our hearts. When we try to be something he didn't intend for us, that's when the trouble starts. Getting back to being bored, how do we know David is bored?

"One evening David Got up from his bed and walked around the roof" (2 Samuel 11:2).

I don't know about you, but if I'm napping in the afternoon, it's a strong indicator that I am bored. Second mistake. When you're bored, find a purpose. Volunteer, take up a hobby, purge the garage—whatever you do, don't wander on your roof. David finds himself encountering the most beautiful woman he has ever seen. Now add to that the "form God gave her is revealed" to David in his first encounter, and you have a bored king on his way to being an active hunter.

From here, the perpetual train wreck of bad decisions begins. Lust leads to pursuit, which leads to conception, which leads to coverup. I find it interesting how David tries to cover up his transgression by getting Uriah to conceive with Bathsheba. Sometimes we attempt to get someone else to compromise their values to cover up something we did.

Uriah refuses to get "special treatment" over his peers, and it costs him his life. This first coverup attempt fails as a result of Uriah's integrity, which causes David to own up to his indiscretion and take accountability for his actions. Actually, that's not what happened. It causes David to escalate his campaign of concealing his indiscretion to murder.

The events that transpire after David takes Bathsheba for his own are an example of what each of us is capable of. I know what you're thinking: *I would never do that! That can't happen to me!* I can promise you David never thought any of this would happen to him. In Phillip Zimbardo's book, *The Lucifer Effect,* we are challenged to accept the idea that if you think you are somehow immune to committing some act, you are probably more susceptible to it than others.

Remember, as Christians, we are not an exception. We are not inoculated from wickedness or evil. As Christians, we are challenged to accept the wickedness of our hearts and surrender it to a loving creator who knows just how to help us overcome it. The thing to remember with regard to David's circumstances is he's not pushing against anything he was not wired to be. He is a man, Bathsheba is a woman, and God wired us to seek after each other. David's sin is obvious to many of us, but keep in mind the attraction to a woman is not sinful; it is the manner and means to which a man desires a woman that is sinful.

This is what Jesus is referring to when he challenges his followers to understand that to think of adultery is to have committed adultery. Had David never laid with Bathsheba but instead plotted in his heart ways to make her his wife, his sin would be no different. Many would say that makes no sense; committing the act is far worse than just plotting. This is how we see cause and consequence.

God sees our thoughts, actions, and outcomes the same way. His way of considering the actions of a person versus the heart of a person is what segregates his way of thinking from ours. God can see the whole picture beginning to end, where we see linear moments that offer feelings only within the confines of the moment they occur. Consider the difference between Saul and David. What elevates David as a king and a leader is the state of his heart. Saul's heart is compromised time and again, and he seeks out his own interest instead of God's. When David seeks out his own interest, he repents and asks God to forgive him for his transgressions. It is always the condition of your heart that matters to God.

GIANTS

David's life is an example of how God often places us in situations to prepare us for his plans. From his anointing to the time he became king was fifteen years. During that time, he was hunted as a fugitive for no reason other than God had chosen him to be king.

David's victories are too numerous to count. His lasting impression on his people is still vivid today. Many of the Jews hoped that Jesus would mirror his reign. They prayed for another warrior king to free them from their oppression. David defeated lions, bears, giants, a psychotic king, and armies too numerous to count but was ultimately defeated by the one thing we all struggle with—ourselves. Sometimes our greatest giant is not the bully in our office or the addiction we are caught up in. It may not even be the temptation that someone other than our spouse can present. The greatest giant we must face is the one that resides in our heart.

Key Reflections

Take time to consider some of the key points of David's life:

- What are some of the giants you have faced in your life or that you are facing now?

- How different is your approach to taking on your giants than David's was to defeating Goliath?

- What giants have defeated you lately, and what can you do to make sure you are victorious next time?

- What does it mean to be a person after God's own heart?

- What parallels do you see between your purpose in God's plan and David's story?

- How can you become the Jonathan for someone else, to help them achieve their purpose in God's plan?

Chapter 6
IDENTITY

THE BIG LEATHER cushions enveloped me as I sat down on the couch in the operations center at the base my father worked at. It was a National Guard weekend, and my dad had brought my sister and me to work. I brought coloring books and puzzles to keep me occupied, but my attention was drawn to the enormous *Jane's Encyclopedia of Aircraft* that sat on the coffee table.

I flipped through page after page, absorbing as much information as I could about aircraft from all over the world. I knew how many pounds of fuel a T-38 could carry by the time I was seven years old. Inevitably, members of my dad's guard unit would walk into the ops center and ask me who I belonged to.

My answer was always the same. "Bull." My dad was given a call sign by his fellow pilots when he started flying. *The Great Santini* starring Robert Duvall was the source of the call sign, from what I was told. The movie is the story of Ben "Bull" Meechum, a marine fighter pilot. The moniker was given to my father because of the striking resemblance my father had to Robert Duvall in the movie.

Upon giving this answer, most people would continue with their day. It was not uncommon to overhear people say, "Whose son is that?" "That's Bull's son." I realized I was Bull's son. I'm not sure any of them knew my name, but they knew I belonged to Bull. It never bothered me as a kid, and even as an adult, I wear the title with a sense of pride.

Not everyone has this opportunity. Sometimes we are thrust into a title or name that we don't choose or receive any pride from. The titles we achieve throughout our lives have an impact on our choices, our thoughts, and our outcomes. Titles don't always tell us who we are, but they give us an idea of where we've been and what others think of us. The nature of titles can impact a delicate aspect of our character and define our identity.

Identity is a complex subject. It has become the focal point of many research studies around the world. Currently, the research suggests that the majority of us begin to form the elements of our identity between the ages of eight and eighteen. This varies from person to person as well as from boys to girls, but essentially, these are the foundational years for generating one's identity. Identity isn't necessarily a "set it and forget it" construct within the human psyche. Identity shifts and alters as you mature. These adjustments become less dramatic the older we get, but regardless of age, our identities modify ever so slightly.

Some of the changes are driven by tragedy, others by revelation, and some are a result of a status we reach. As an example, consider Susan. Susan is eight. She loves dolls and horses and dreams of owning a horse one day. She plays pretend with her stuffed horse, Milo. It's not uncommon to see Susan feeding and watering Milo and even putting him in bed when he doesn't feel well. Her mother is a doctor who lets her borrow her stethoscope whenever Milo needs a checkup.

By twelve, Milo is still a fixture in Susan's life, but the interactions have changed. She holds Milo when she watches TV or sleeps next to him at night, but the make-believe isn't what it used to be. Susan still loves horses and has now plastered posters of horses all over her room. Her focus has become friendships. Girlfriends, sleepovers, hair, and nails take a front row to Milo. Her social standing among her peer group has become a priority. Acceptance, fitting in, and standing out all at the same time are critical. She begins to adopt trends and form her own to finish a physical and mental image of herself.

By sixteen, her identity is driven more and more by her peers. Boys become a factor in altering Susan's identity. She sees celebrities, rock stars, actors, and athletes and begins to associate these individuals with hopes that she has about her future.

She may alter her clothing or her hair to gain the attention of a certain boy at school. Then she changes it back when her heart is broken by said boy. She may even take up a new hobby. Academics become important to Susan. She focuses on getting good grades because she wants to be identified as being smart.

At eighteen, Susan has college brain. *Where do I go? What do I study? How much is this going to cost?* These questions play on repeat in her mind. As she enters college, the identity alteration starts all over again. New friends, new trends, new hobbies, and plenty of boys.

Susan's identity has morphed from dolls to dates, from dress up to dress shopping, and from little stuffed Milo to Miley. The changes to Susan's identity come slower and less dramatically, save for those life-altering events. Careers, marriage, children, and the loss of loved ones all have an impact.

I often tell my wife, if I could meet myself when I was fifteen, the encounter would not end well. I would kick that kid up one side of the street and down the other. Candy bars and soda for breakfast? What was I thinking? The identity I have now doesn't see eye to eye with the identity I had at fifteen. My priorities, obligations, and seasons of life have altered who I am and what I identify with. So, what delineates identity from a fad? How do we isolate the elements of our identity from a fleeting trend? It's all about change and purpose.

GIFT

The nature of identity and how it manifests makes it apparent that identity is a gift from God. This gift allows us to set ourselves apart from one another. It allows us to assimilate traits of others and alter our course toward a specific outcome in our future. As if it were an unseen fingerprint, it allows us to delineate our place among the ocean of social encounters we navigate throughout our lives. Our society emphasizes, as it does with many gifts from God, identity in all the wrong ways. In our culture, people think that identity is somehow relegated to your salary and your appearance. This robs us of God's intention for identity.

The book of Esther provides us with a unique perspective on the response to less than ideal circumstances. This is one of only two female perspectives we find in the Old Testament. This is the compelling story of a young woman orphaned as a child and raised by her cousin, only to become the savior of the Jewish people. Esther's identity is complicated. She is raised in a home that is not that of her parents. The loss of parents at such a young age has deep, lasting impacts on a person's identity. Losing my mother at age nine altered the trajectory of my life dramatically.

Esther has two names, Hadassah and Esther. The text is not descriptive as to why or how she was given two names. There is some evidence to suggest that the name change had to do with living under Persian rule. I can only imagine the complexities of being known by one name for so much of your life, only to be called something completely different. Add to this the political and cultural backdrop to Esther's environment, and you have an entirely new set of issues that impact her and solidify her place in the world.

During Esther's life, the Jews are occupied by a Persian king by the name of Xerxes. He has conquered most of the known world and has vast wealth and a large kingdom made up of many different cultures and people, the Jews being only one of these groups. Imagine being thrust into another culture. The language, clothing, and traditions are all different from your own. Consider what it must be like for a young girl to be raised in this dual climate of Jewish tradition and Persian rule. Ideas, beliefs, and heritage clash daily.

We come back to this idea of dual citizenship that we discussed in earlier chapters. Esther was a Jew, but she was living in a Persian world. As Christians, we experience the same duality. Our beliefs often clash with mainstream society. When pro-life, family values, and accountability become talking points in America, Christians are vilified as intolerant villains with nothing more than an agenda to dictate the terms of another's life. We are not unlike Esther, strangers in a strange land.

DETAILS

God's providence is always in the details. Reading scripture is often entertaining, frequently enthralling, and sometimes monotonous. As much as I have heard "the devil is in the details," I would argue that when it comes to scripture, God is in the details. The backdrop of the book of Esther is compelling and often overlooked. What you see with regard to the cultural and political climate in the book of Esther is God and Satan working for the souls of humanity. We have antagonists like Haman. We have protagonists like Mordecai and Esther. But it's the characters we don't see and who aren't even mentioned who are moving these characters across the stage for their own purposes.

Satan has elegantly used Haman, the descendant of Agag, an Amalekite, to be second in command to Xerxes. God has placed Mordecai as charge over Esther "at such a time as this," to be the savior of all God's people. Remember, Agag was the king of the Amalekites who Saul was supposed to kill and didn't until after misfortune befell him and the Jews. The neglect of God's will for our lives has long-lasting impacts for not only our future but those of the generations that will follow us.

Despite Saul's disobedience and the circumstances that present themselves to Esther and Mordecai, God always keeps his promises. Mordecai is aware of God's promise to the Jews. He makes it clear to Esther that even if she doesn't advocate on behalf of God's people, salvation will come from another place (Esther 4:14).

Nowhere in the book of Esther is the word God used. Yet his presence is so overwhelming in the story that to mention him might be considered redundant. Esther's courage is demonstrated in her request of the Jewish people and her participation in fasting for three days prior to engaging the king.

This is surrender, surrendering the outcome to God. In verse 16 of chapter 4, she makes it clear, "if I perish, I perish." It's easy to get attached to the outcome, especially when our lives are on the line. This is also the case with identity. When we feel God's nudging, prodding, and poking to surrender a piece of ourselves to him, we are resistant and afraid.

Maybe it's surrendering something we find trivial, like spending too much time on our phones, or maybe it's something more challenging to surrender, like drinking, pornography, or the attention of someone who is not our spouse. These things draw us in and change the way we feel about ourselves. They give us a sense of empowerment.

When God asks us to surrender these things, he's not asking for anything short of our hearts. He witnesses your heart being occupied by things that take you from his presence and seeks relentlessly to free you from it. When we surrender these aspects of ourselves, we are performing surgery on our identity. *Who am I without this? What will happen to my relationships? Will my wife still love me?* These are all questions that dominate our minds when we feel like God is asking us to surrender something that has taken root in our heart. Esther provides us with at least one strategy to overcome these concerns.

HAMBURGER

I have wrestled with fasting for many years. I have often thought it wasn't necessary or meaningful. The truth is quite the contrary. Biblically, we are called to fast even in the presence of Christ's salvation (Mark 2:20). Fasting is a form of surrender at the most primal level of our existence.

When we consider Maslow's hierarchy of needs, food is right there on the ground level. Imagine a juicy hamburger with all the right toppings. The first bite is savory and salty in all the right ways. Now consider not eating for the next three days. See how hard that is. Fasting gives us a glimpse into what it means to surrender, to forego something that is essential to our survival and recognize we are doing it to honor God.

When fasting, you will find yourself relying on God to overcome the temptation of downing those french fries or that hamburger. It encourages you to seek him in those moments of weakness. Next time you feel like there is something God is asking you to surrender, take a day and fast a few meals in that day. Instead of eating during that time, get out a devotional and spend time in prayer with God. You might be surprised how satisfying spending time with God can be.

BEAUTY

During my study of Esther, the circumstances she was in and how she came to find herself in those circumstances began to weigh heavily on my heart. Young girl, beauty contest, not much choice in the matter or the outcome. There's an elephant in this chapter that is obviously used in God's plan for Esther and Xerxes, but our culture finds it difficult to accept. Esther is beautiful. We read it over and over in this short book. Today we see beauty compromised—Photoshopped and digitally enhanced and altered. We see an emphasis on the aesthetics of others and for all the wrong reasons.

God provided each of us with the faculties to witness and discern beauty. All that is beautiful he created. So, what happened to beauty as God intended and beauty as our culture experiences it? God uses Esther's beauty to save his people. What does this tell us? God can use anything to fulfill his providential will. We use beauty to sell products we don't need, that don't work, to people who can't afford them, so they can feel even more self-conscious about their image than they already do. We use things for our personal indulgence. What if we looked at this differently?

Consider a mountain scene. Perhaps a valley with a crystal blue lake nestled between two snowcapped mountains. What you see is beautiful. It's God's creation. How can this scene be any better? What if you were there standing on the shore of that lake? The wind blows ever so gently as the sun warms your face. You take a deep breath in and smell the fresh pine trees. The sound of the water as it meets and retreats from the shore soothes you. Perhaps you are there sharing this with a loved one, taking it all in together. There is no need to speak, just time to be quiet and enjoy God's creation. What would make this better? If it were real. If you were experiencing it in the moment, as it's happening to you. The beauty in this moment is not just what you see, it's also what you don't see. Much of the beauty you are experiencing standing on that shore is in the sensation, the feelings, the smells, and the sounds. This is the true beauty that Esther possessed.

Xerxes was a conqueror, a strong man ruling over thousands of people. Governed by an insatiable desire to see his rule and kingdom expand, nothing would stand in his way—save for a little Jewish girl with a beautiful heart. Esther's heart and all of who she was captured Xerxes. Beauty on the inside is what captivates us and makes us want to be present with that person.

Just like the mountains, all that is occurring in the moment brings down our walls and makes us know we belong and that we never want to leave. Jesus emphasized and personified this very characteristic. He challenged people's hearts, the way they spoke, how they treated others. God can use anything to fulfill his purpose for your life. He's challenged each of us to let the beauty of our hearts show brighter than the beauty we hold on the outside. When the world can experience his love through our lives is truly when we bring the beauty of his kingdom to a world that desperately needs it.

Key Reflections

Take time to consider some of the key points of Esther's life:

- How would you describe your identity?

- Are there pieces of your identity that God wants you to surrender?

- What does beautiful mean to you?

- What is the hardest thing you have had to give up?

- What do you see as the difference between God's purpose for beauty and how people have used it?

Chapter 7

VICTIM

"THERE ARE NO victims in this classroom!" I remember watching that scene over and over from the critically acclaimed movie *Dangerous Minds*. Michelle Pfeiffer's character challenges her students on the choices they have and the choices they make. Choices are a by-product of circumstance. This is to say the situation you find yourself in determines the choices available to you. I remember my daughter and I having a discussion one night about why God lets bad things happen to good people.

My wife and I adopted Kylie when she was twelve years old. Her question was not out of place considering what she had been through in the first twelve years of her life. As a I sat on her bed, I remember having one of my infamous drive-by prayers. Drive-by prayers are those moments when you are significantly outnumbered on the spiritual front and the situation is time sensitive. As I listened to this young girl's heart, my inner dialogue went something like this.

God ... little help here!

Almost immediately, the response came as if I had known the answer all along. As she looked at me waiting for a response to a legitimate question, I said, "God doesn't interfere with the free will of the people in our lives. He made his promise to each of us that our choice belonged to us. Just as he gave Adam and Eve a choice, he gave each of us a choice as well."

She looked at me with a sense of understanding. I continued. "God may not interfere in the free will of others, but he is really good at making ugly things that people do remarkably beautiful. The trick is we have to surrender those things to him."

There have been a few moments when I felt like everything had come together as God ordained it—such as sitting on that bed, hearing those words come out of my mouth, and knowing deep down they weren't my own. I was merely a conduit between that sweet little girl and an almighty God. I kissed her on the forehead and said good night. As I walked out of her bedroom, it all made sense. All the tragedy and pain of the life I had led up to that point, all the suffering my wife and I had endured, God was using it all for this little girl.

Each tear we had ever cried, each moment we screamed in anguish was going to be used to help this young girl. Ask me if it was worth it. Ask me if I'd suffer through it all over again. Absolutely. God doesn't waste our pain. Our suffering breaks his heart, and he refuses to let one tear fall in vain. We hold our pain. We carry it like some sort of badge of honor.

How many friends or colleagues do we share our tragedy with, only to find their words of sympathy empty and hollow? As if by sharing it with them, they can somehow assuage our grief. It's a tall order to ask of anyone. They have their own grief and tragedy to endure. How does God use our pain for his glory? Well, it just so happens we have quite a compelling story of tragedy at the hands of others.

There are few things that get me worked up. I am objective when it comes to most things. I may get upset at first, but I typically try to consider as many reasons as I can for why something might have happened. Whereas finding empty potato chip bags in the pantry or half-drank bottles of water strewn throughout the house might raise my blood pressure, there are several taboo choices that test the limits of my Christianity.

Animal abuse, child neglect, and overall injustice send me into bitter diatribes and tirades that I have become known for. It's the senselessness of these choices that sends me off the deep end. It's something I am actively working through in my walk. How do I be still in moments of discomfort? Why do I lack faith when the going gets tough? How do I praise God when other people's choices cause me pain?

God has a way of providing us answers in the most irrefutable of ways. He acknowledges our difficulty and suffering and then asks us to let him use that pain for his glory. This is obviously represented in the life of Christ, but is this not the theme of many stories in the Bible? It just so happens to be the theme of one of my favorite stories, the story of Joseph.

FAVORITE

What does it mean to be a favorite? What are some of your favorite things? Favorite is a tough one. It implies there is more than one to choose from and requires a choice that elevates one above the rest. What's your favorite movie? What's your favorite song? Which is your favorite child? Tough questions. Joseph was a favorite child (Genesis 37:3). Not only was he a favorite child, he was the favorite among twelve kids. Joseph was Rachel's son, and Rachel was Jacob's favorite wife. It follows that Joseph would be the favorite child. Well, maybe not the best logic, especially when you consider what favoritism did to Jacob when he was a child.

Despite Jacob's past, he elevated Joseph to this title and made him a coat so that everyone would know it. How did Reuben know he wasn't the favorite, despite being the eldest son of Jacob? Well, he didn't have the favorite coat. This coat was the equivalent of Jacob buying Joseph a brand-new, shiny red Ferrari, while the other boys road their bikes to and from school.

There was nothing subtle about this gift. Not only did Jacob want Joseph to know he was his favorite, he wanted everyone else to know as well. So, Joseph being the conscientious type, could have decided to accept the coat graciously and pack it away in his locker so that his brothers don't have to constantly be reminded of where they sit in the pecking order. Not the case. No, Joseph decides to flaunt that coat like the bright, shiny Ferrari it was—in front of his brothers, in front of his friends, in front of everyone. As if being the favorite son wasn't enough, Joseph had a gift—the gift of dreams.

Don't underestimate dreams. God uses them on several occasions to convey his truth. Joseph not only had dreams but was able to make sense of them.

I often wonder what he'd say about my dreams. Somehow my dreams always have my wife and kids leaving me in random places by accident, never on purpose. Not as compelling as the dreams Joseph had. Just as much as Joseph seemed incapable of keeping his status among the children quiet, he had a problem with putting his foot in his mouth. Joseph shared his dreams, and one of those dreams was the straw the broke the camel's back. According to the account in Genesis, Joseph dreams of him ruling over his brothers and them bowing down to him—probably not the dream you want to go flaunting about to your already disenfranchised brothers. But not Joseph. He was cocky to a fault, even to the point where he set his dear old dad off (Genesis 37:10).

We all have limits. "A man has got to know his limitations," as Clint Eastwood so elegantly put it, through squinty eyes and pursed lips. Joseph's choices set forth a course of action that would change the trajectory of history forever. It's hard being the favorite. If there is any takeaway from this part of the story, it would be that if you're the favorite, take comfort in knowing it and just keep your mouth shut.

HUMBLED

It's easy to praise God when things are going well. If you're like me, you constantly find your offerings to God feeble and broken. You take comfort in knowing that God sees your heart in the effort. I often think about the drawings my grandkids bring me and how I rejoice in finding the effort in the struggle of each drawing. I equate my praise to God as something akin to these colorful drawings. I can't quite make out what it is, but I know the intention and the effort that were in it from the start. I'm grateful God gives us a glimpse of his experience with us through the experience we have with our children.

It's not always easy to praise God when all the colors in our picture begin to run together. When all the colors bleed together, the result is something dark and disgusting. How do we take that and still offer it to God?

The answer comes in analyzing the catalyst for the circumstance. Who caused the colors to bleed together? Sometimes it's us, and other times it's someone else who got a hold of our picture and our crayons. Sometimes we get carried away with our understanding of the tragedy that befell us. Too often, we seek revenge or retaliation when we are suffering at the hand of others. What should we do instead? Well, consider Joseph's situation. Brothers plot to kill him. I'm not saying he deserved it, but I get the frustration. Maybe stuff him in a locker for a few minutes; death seems a little permanent. God's right there listening to this plot, and his plans will not be derailed. One brother has the sense to sell Joseph. What do you do when your brothers' plot to kill you turns into you being sold as a slave instead? You praise God.

LOYALTY

My son-in-law is quite the young man. He's been through a lot in a short time. He has an enormous heart. He's the kind of guy you can tell has so much love in him he doesn't quite know what to do with all of it. He's rarely been given the tools to know how to talk about what he feels. Young men today aren't celebrated for being emotionally in tune. Despite this, he does the absolute best he can with what he has. With eleven years of service in the US Air Force, he's a proud father of a girl and a boy, Kenna and Ronen.

As a father and a husband, he's a force to be reckoned with, and he has become the true meaning behind Proverbs 27:17 in my life. He is an answer to prayer for our daughter Courtney, our grandkids, and for me. He's loyal in ways that aren't typically seen in our modern culture. He has devoted himself to making every effort to help his mom and his siblings in every way he can, despite his circumstances. Whenever I think of Joseph, I think of my son-in-law Kevin.

Joseph shows loyalty to God in ways that outperform even what many of the disciples of Jesus did. When you're sold into slavery, it's quite the blow to your ego. Nothing you have belongs to you. The air you breathe is that of your masters. The beating of your heart is on loan from the one who owns you. Each step you take is guided by a leash attached to your mind. The one thing a slave has that no master can take from him is his soul. Joseph knew that as a slave, he was now a man bought and paid for, his life no longer his own.

From coats to shackles, from dreams to nightmares, from favorite to forgotten, his life would never be the same. The only thing that remained of his old life was his faith in an almighty God who had a purpose for his pain and a plan for his life. When the world grabs a hold of you, grab a hold of God and watch what he is capable of. Joseph realized that if he was going to be a slave, he was going to be the best slave, and in so doing, he honored God. When we show up well in the midst of our tragedy, we honor God. People notice when you have something in your tragedy that they don't.

Suffering as a result of another always hurts. Whether it's abuse by a parent or abuse by a spouse, the pain is unique because of the position these people hold in our lives. They are the ones who are supposed to be our advocates or cheerleaders, our encouragers. When they choose to cause us pain, they are the antithesis of all we hoped they would be. That creates a kind of pain that only those who have experienced it can relate to. It's the kind of pain Christ died for.

Judas's betrayal is no accident. The scourging Jesus endured is not for dramatic affect. All of it has purpose. It lets us know he suffered the way we do—not just in the betrayal or the physical abuse but at the point that our heart shatters as a result of those we love causing us pain. What do you do with that pain? Where do you put it? How do you reconcile the gap between who people should be in your life and who they truly are?

Consider if Joseph spent his days as a slave feeling pity for himself, plotting revenge on his brothers. God's work never gets done in our pity or our revenge. Joseph surrendered all his pain to God and began to fulfill God's purpose for his life one day at a time. This is a great deal easier to type than it is to practice, but trust me—God moves mountains of pain to get to the center of your heart.

Ever been accused of something you know you didn't do? *I did not eat the last brownie! I swear! I put the toilet seat down. I know I did! There were still chips left in that bag when I put it back in the pantry.* I remember feeling the need to defend myself when I was younger. It's hard to convince people when you don't have an advocate.

As I got older, I started gaining a great deal of peace from *let your yes be yes and your no be no.* I knew the truth of what I had done and didn't do, and whether people wanted to believe that or not made no difference to me.

Being accused of something, depending on the severity of it, can be a debilitating moment in a person's life. Your family members may begin to doubt your story. Your friends may become distant upon hearing what you are accused of. It can be a lonely place, especially when you know the truth.

I often think about the incident between Joseph and Potiphar's wife and how frustrating that had to have been—working so hard to be the best you can be, only to have it snatched away from you by some indecent woman.

The story speaks of the evidence brought against Joseph, his coat that was left behind. *I'm detecting a theme: colored coat gets my brothers to sell me into slavery, and now this coat gets me accused of rape.* I think I'd learn to live with being cold if I was Joseph.

Throughout all that befalls Joseph, there is a constant sense that he trusts God with his circumstances. I can almost hear his prayers. *God, if this what you have for me, show me your will. I will honor you no matter where my path may lead.* I pray that I can be more like Joseph when trouble comes my way.

What's unfortunate is I am still bad at it, and my misfortune looks like a Disneyland vacation compared to Joseph's problems—sold into slavery, worked hard to become the favorite again, only to be accused of rape and sent to prison. Where do you go from there?

TRUE LOVE

God doesn't forsake us. He is quiet, and he is still, but he is always with us. During our greatest terror, he is there watching and weeping with us. He has promises to keep to all of us. Our free will and that of everyone else is a commitment he made to his creation. Love without freedom isn't love at all.

My wife and I could be anywhere in the world—our jobs permit us to work remotely from anywhere—yet I choose to be here, right where she is. I have the freedom to go anywhere and be with anyone, but I choose her above all others. That's how real love exists. Such is the case between God and his creation.

The greatest love must be chosen freely without demands. God gives us that choice and loves us despite our disobedience and our sin. With that commitment to free will, God must allow others to make choices that affect us in horrifying ways. Just as Joseph suffered at the hands of his brothers and Potiphar's wife, so to do we suffer at the hands of our family, friends, and strangers. The difficult part is honoring God in the presence of our suffering.

We often blame God for not intervening, for not stopping the abuse, the affair, the death of a loved one. I think, however, if we stopped and looked at what love requires, we wouldn't want a love with our creator that wasn't real. Absolutely we want the pain to stop, the heartache to end, the suffering to subside, but at what cost? To feel the greatest love, we must be willing to accept the pain that comes with it. The cross provides the most succinct picture of this concept. The suffering he endured for us was the cost for the love he had for each of us.

Think of the depth of pain you would be willing to suffer for your family. What you feel, what drives you to that answer is the love you have for them. True love comes with a cost, and to embrace that cost means leaving it in God's hands to create something beautiful. Joseph did just that. He continued to rely on God, knowing that in the end God would be glorified through his suffering.

PERSONAL PRISON

Prison may be the most unlikely place you could ever consider yourself being. Prisons are not always made of concrete and steel. Some are the products of our own design, while others are the result of those around us. I have listened to people who are imprisoned by their own greed and selfishness, and others are in prisons created by the relationships they have.

These personal prisons manifest differently from one situation to another, from one person to another. The way we enter and exit them is different as well. Being tried and convicted of a crime planted Joseph in a prison virtually overnight. The prisons we create for ourselves have an intake process that can last years. The process is so slow and gradual that it's too late before we realize it. While it may require a parole board and mercy on behalf of the courts to free someone from a physical prison, leaving the prisons of our own creation requires much more.

STARTING OVER

Joseph again finds himself in a circumstance because of someone else's choices. Despite having made so much progress in Potiphar's household, he now finds himself starting over at the bottom of society. Starting over is not something we're unfamiliar with. Divorce, layoffs, and the death of a loved one can put us in a place of feeling like we have to start over. Each of us, like Joseph, works to enhance our lives. We strive, sacrifice, and claw our ways to the top of our ascribed and achieved statuses.

Our efforts are to build our kingdom with family, friends, careers, and our passions. Life delivers unexpected circumstances. I cannot tell you how many times I have met people who have undergone hardship, and their response is, "I never thought something like this could happen to me." This seems to be more often the case with Christians. Somehow, we believe that by pursuing God in our daily lives, we become inoculated from hardship and tragedy. We spend our time shouting, "Why me?" Often the greatest achievements in human history are birthed out of tragedy and hardship. Joseph just happens to be one example.

What do you do after being number one twice in your life, only to have someone else take you to the bottom? Well, if you are Joseph, you praise God. Every choice you make, with every person you meet, you illuminate God and all his glory. You throw down the trivial, the selfish pride and tantrums, and replace them with seeking God above else and honoring him in the presence of all the hurt and pain. You stop blaming others and God for your circumstances and instead shout, "Not my will but yours, Father."

Joseph's story is an example of how the scars from our past become tools in the hands of an almighty God who refuses to allow our suffering to go in vain. His glory will vindicate you and bring your enemies to their knees. You commit to God's providential will and surrender your own so that he might use you to move mountains, despite your fragile existence.

Joseph wasn't a slave or a prisoner; he was an ambassador to the world for God. This is something he knew and reminded himself of every day. When life brought him storms, he sought God's purpose in each drop of rain. He knew that through each trial, he was becoming the key that God needed him to be to unlock his purpose in Gods' plan.

FORGIVEN

The first time I read through Joseph's story in Genesis, I was overwhelmed by feelings of grief and joy. Joseph's tragic circumstances conjured thoughts of revenge and retaliation. I couldn't wait to hear how God was going to punish the evil parties in this story. I knew that the final chapter of this story was going to make what happened to Sodom and Gomorra look like a child's nursery rhyme. Brothers of Joseph all hunted down one by one and meeting their demise in one creative way after another. Potiphar's wife would be exposed as the harlot she was. In all my creative ideas of how this story should end, I never came close to the actual outcome. The outcomes for Joseph, for his brothers, and for me are ones only God could weave.

As a culture, we don't discuss forgiveness in depth. Sure, we all want to be forgiven, and at some level, we acknowledge we need to forgive others, but many of us don't come to terms with the necessity for forgiveness. We hold onto grudges, plot revenge, and suffer in silence while our transgressors sleep soundly each night. Unforgiveness is dangerous, and God knows what it does to us as his creation. It robs us of joy, peace, faith, and love. When we wallow in the depth of how we have been wronged, we set up mansions for the enemy to take up residency in our hearts. Joseph would never have been able to accomplish half of what he did for Potiphar or for Pharaoh if he had held onto hatred for his brothers.

Joseph could have punished his brothers, and many of us would have seen no fault in him. Punishing his brothers for what they had done would not have changed them. Consider the change in his brothers upon being forgiven. The beauty of the reunion between Joseph and his brothers is in how he sets his brothers free not just from their act against him but their act against God.

> But as for you, you meant evil against me; but God meant it for good, in order to bring it about as it is this day, to save many people alive. (Genesis 50:20 NKJV)

How do we unpack this? First, acknowledge the actions of others: "you meant evil against me." Acknowledge God's outcome of that action by others: "but God meant it for good." Describe in what way God fulfilled his purpose: "to save many people alive." Joseph had already been set free from the anger and hatred his brothers' actions had caused him. He had given that to God years ago. It was now time to set his brothers free from their prisons.

As I write this, I think about the people in my life I have wronged, those I have taken advantage of, and I pray that God might have used my selfish actions for his purpose in that person's life. It is the stuff that our prayer lives should include. *Father, I acknowledge my selfish acts against others and how those actions have caused others pain and anguish. I pray that you help me to understand how the things I do hurt others, and I ask that your will be done in their lives despite the harm I have brought them.*

Joseph's story resonates at a deep level for us. We are both Joseph and the brothers in this story. We have all been wronged and wrong others. In the brothers' redemption, we seek our own. We aspire to Joseph's triumph over his circumstances. Regardless of what season we are in, God has a purpose and a plan for all the suffering we endure and all the heartache we create.

Key Reflections

Take a moment and consider how Joseph's story speaks to God's purpose for your life:

- Have you ever been the favorite or know someone in your family who is?

- How do you accept either being the favorite or having to live with not being the favorite?

- Have you ever been sold out by people you trusted?

- Have you ever sold anyone else out?

- What are the prisons you find yourself in right now?

- Are these prisons you created or that someone else created?

- Write these prisons down and identify what impact they are having on your present and on your future.

- What is God's intention for forgiveness?

Chapter 8
PRIDE

I SAT IN THE uncomfortable plastic chair as I heard my fellow classmates' names called. Each one stood up and walked to the front of the room. They were handed a plaque, and after a handshake and a smile for the camera, they went back to their seats. "Deputy Sheriff Middagh!" I gave a nod to my dad, sitting next to me, as I got up and walked to the front of the room. It was my AZ POST (Arizona Peace Officer Standards Training) graduation.

Maricopa County Sheriff's Office has a volunteer program known as the MCSO Posse. It is predominately made up of retirees and career folks who are looking to give back to their community. Posse members assist deputies with traffic duties, administrative work, and security details. My father had joined the posse and encouraged me to do so. At the time, I was working on getting a job in law enforcement, so volunteering with MCSO made sense.

As I walked to the front, I kept reminding myself, *Grab with the left, shake with the right, smile for the camera.* As I reached the front of the room, my training officer smiled at me and presented my plaque. I got the whole "grab with left, shake with right" part correct; it was the "smile for the camera" that I messed up. So, most of the pictures from my graduation are profile shots of me smiling at my training officer.

I remember how proud I was in that moment and how proud my dad was. It was truly the first time in my life I felt like he was really proud of me. Pride is a funny thing. I have a love-hate relationship with it. It's like sugar. I love sugar, especially ice cream, but I know it's bad for me. I never wanted to be a prideful person. In some cases, situations and circumstances in our lives make it almost unavoidable to be proud. Daughter brings home straight A's. Son hits his first homerun. Daughter gets married. Son gets first big promotion. These events just create pride in us; it's almost unavoidable. This got me to thinking, How should pride manifest? What is God's intention for pride? Do we have examples of good and bad pride in the Bible?

> And behold, a voice from heaven said, "This is
> my beloved Son, with whom I am well pleased."
> (Matthew 3:17 ESV)

This account in Matthew, following Jesus's baptism, is an indication that God is and can be proud. In this case, he is proud of his son. This tells me that the feeling of pride and the situations that create pride in us are a gift from God. Like many other gifts from God—*cough*, sugar—where it goes wrong is in its excess. Pride in the moment is a natural and healthy response to an observed outcome.

We see an outcome that aligns to our hope, and our hope is realized in that moment. We have hope for ourselves, our children, our family, and our friends. When the stars align in their lives and they achieve a desired outcome, hope is set free, and pride takes its place.

So where does pride go wrong? The danger with pride is twofold. First, pride can blind us to the truth about ourselves and others. Second, pride is often used to cover our insecurities. Pride for pride's sake is something I see in many parents. *Because they are my son or daughter, I am proud of them, and somehow this covers a multitude of sins committed by said son or daughter.* Being authentic with our children, ourselves, and our friends cultivates substantial relationships. Pride can get in the way of that, and it leaves our relationships built on a compromised foundation.

Every one of us has encountered individuals who have misplaced pride. These are the people who like to recite their résumé to you as if they are in a perpetual job interview. You have heard how they graduated top of their class—or would have, had it not been for an unfair professor. They speak of their accolades as if they are attempting to convince us of their academic, physical, or professional achievements. Additionally, they are repetitive; they will share the same achievement multiple times on different occasions. If you introduce them to someone, they will be sure to besiege them with their adventures and accomplishments, whether solicited or not.

When I encounter these people, I often attempt to uncover what's driving the necessity to deliver such a laundry list of trophies. I did not ask for their history of triumphs. So, what is it? Well, it typically boils down to a number of factors. Personality type, birth order, or a relationship with a parent or mentor might be the driving force behind this ceaseless endeavor sharing. Their need to have others be impressed or proud is an attempt to cover their insecurities. Don't misunderstand. There is nothing wrong with being proud of climbing Mount Everest or swimming the English Channel. It's the desire to share those details unsolicited where the pride highway takes a wrong turn.

Pride used in the right way elevates others and yourself. When your child or a friend shares with you an accomplishment, sharing in their pride is meaningful and is one ingredient in the recipe for healthy relationships. The children of parents who have never heard the words "I'm proud of you" will tell you the doubt and emptiness that can create in a young child's mind. So, pride, like many gifts from God, can used for both good and bad. The important question is, How does pride help us to understand God's purpose for our lives?

FISHERMAN

Peter was a man among men. I often imagine Peter as the kind of guy who takes up a lot of space even though he may not be very tall, the kind of guy who demands an audience. Probably the kind of guy who, when he walked in a room, people noticed—charismatic, charming, outspoken, and opinionated. I'm sure he had the ears of many of his fellow fishermen. He made compelling arguments and always had something to say about the subject being discussed. He may have only been a fisherman, but I guarantee you it mattered to him.

So, what compels an outspoken, boisterous extrovert to follow a stranger? Somebody even more dynamic. The dynamic types are usually good at picking out those who are like them. When confronted by Jesus's offer, Peter felt compelled to respond with a big gesture.

> "Come, follow me," Jesus said, "and I will send you
> out to fish for people." (Matthew 4:19 NIV)

Peter heard the "and I will send you out to fish for people"; this would appeal to an extrovert. The social types love to be surrounded by people. Who was this man, and what was he speaking of, fishing for men? Whatever it was, Peter had to know more. Leaving that boat and those nets behind altered the course of his life and history forever. Sometimes our purpose requires only one small act of faith, and in that moment, the world will never be the same.

What does it take for us to act on faith? The degree of faith that is required is different for each of us. For example, if some stranger asked me to leave everything I have behind and follow him, I'm not so sure I have that much faith. I'd like to think I do, but I'm not so sure.

How hard we cling to something determines the level of faith required. For some of us, tithing becomes a huge faith issue. For my wife, it was a challenge for many years, and God called her out. I think it was the verse in Malachi 3:10 that really got her over the faith hurdle. For others, the faith requirement gets steep when it comes to our children, our spouses, or our careers. Surrendering or altering how we see these things in our lives requires tremendous faith. Ironically, are they not the same things we gain pride from?

I think Peter's pride drove him to follow Jesus. I think he saw this whole fisher-of-men idea as a challenge. Fishing can be quite daunting. I have a feeling Peter was exceptional at his trade and was ready for a new challenge. Whatever drove him to trade in his nets for the Gospel, we are all the better for it.

Following Peter through the Gospels, we get one of the best character profiles of any of the disciples. No other disciple is more front and center than Peter. From the challenging questions to the jockeying for position in the kingdom of God, to the cutting off a guard's ear, Peter is a character suited for any of the greatest novels in history. He is dynamic and cunning, intelligent and loyal, all the things an author needs in a protagonist. Peter is the disciple who we see do the most and, save for Judas, fall the hardest. So, what can we attribute to Peter's success and failure?

NAME

Names matter. As we talked about in the chapter exploring Esther, it is one of the first gifts we receive from our parents. Jesus starts his relationship with Peter by establishing a role for Peter. He has a clear purpose for Peter, and that requires a bit of an identity shift. Jesus bestows upon Peter not so much a name but a title—Petros or rock. I'm sure to Peter this was insulting or, if nothing else, confusing. Imagine if a stranger asked you to follow them, and the first exchange of your relationship was that you would be forever referred to as "rock." Not the most compelling way to secure a friendship.

There's pride in a name. It means something to us. Little did Peter know the impact this name change would have on him or his character. If you want to be something, you have to believe it first. Muhammad Ali spoke about how he had to first tell himself he was the greatest before it could ever be true.

Jesus telling Peter that he was to have a new name and the reason why drives Peter's nature to take pride in not only the new name but the purpose behind it. Jesus is using Peter's nature to fulfill God's plan. In this case, he is altering Peter's frame of identity to establish a new person, one on which the church would find its foundation.

> And I tell you that you are Peter, and on this rock,
> I will build my church, and the gates of Hades will
> not overcome it. (Matthew 16:18 NIV)

God made each of us and knows our nature. He knows in what way he can take the nature you have and form it into something he can use to reach people for his kingdom. Never underestimate how your nature can be used by God to change lives—and in some cases, history.

RIGHT-HAND MAN

Men are interesting creatures. God made men curious. They typically have a streak of mischief. John Eldredge's book *Wild at Heart* does a fantastic job outlining the nature of both little boys and men. What happens when you get twelve men together with the son of God? Well, the need for structure takes over.

Male social groups typically have a leader—someone who is charismatic, slow to judge, a risk-taker, witty, and a people person. The leader here in this group is preordained. Jesus fit the profile for the leader of these twelve men. Once the leader is established, a natural hierarchy begins to form.

We have heard of alpha males and the social dynamics that surround them. Peter was an alpha personality. He knew he couldn't hold a flame to Jesus, but he wanted to establish his place in the pecking order of the disciples. How does one go about doing this? Well, first you ask the right questions, and then you give the right answers to the questions you are being asked. The beauty of Peter's character is how his humility and pride take center stage at the same time. When asked by Jesus, "Who do you say that I am?" his answer is humble and respectful.

> Simon Peter answered, "You are the Messiah, the Son of the living God." (Matthew 16:16 NIV)

It's a beautiful and well-crafted response. Where did Peter get such an awesome answer? Talk about getting the answers to the test. This wasn't Peter looking over the shoulder of the disciple next to him or copying the answer sheet. This was the equivalent of having the principal of the school coming to tell you the answer.

Way to go, Peter! Great answer! Way to score some points toward that promotion of right-hand man to Jesus. Oh, but wait. It doesn't count. God gave you the answer. The truth is it counts more than if he had come up with the answer on his own. Having God reveal to Peter the identity of Jesus was a strong indicator that God liked the cut of his jib. If that isn't something worth being proud of, what is?

DO YOU LOVE ME?

Relationships are complex. They require a sense of understanding about the role that each person plays and how that role highlights the other's strengths and mitigates the other's weaknesses. This is the case between Peter and Jesus. Few relationships can exist in the absence of some form of love. Regardless of the makeup of the relationship, a love for each other must be present for that relationship to flourish. The relationship we have with our spouse is often the one most categorized with love.

Every February, we are bombarded by commercials and pink parades of flowers and cards in every grocery store. Romantic love is a natural element in our society, but it comprises only a small percentage of the love we experience throughout our lives. The love we have for our children, our parents, and our friends all articulate differently than romantic love. Despite this, we have only one word for love in the English language.

I can say, "I love you," to my wife and my daughter, and they mean very different things. Think about the relationships you have and how the love you have for each of the people in those relationships is different. What about how each of them loves you? First John 4:8 tells us that God is love. It should be no surprise that the love we feel for others and the love we feel in return shows up in so many ways.

My children have never asked me if I love them. Nor has my wife. I'd like to think this is a testament to my reassuring them that I do. I think it has more to do with how secure my family is, and as a result, they don't find it necessary to solicit my love. So, what do you do when the son of God asks you, "Do you love me?" My answer is easy. Fall on your knees, bury your face in the sand, and plead with him to hear your heart and the love it has for him.

Peter took a different approach. When the question came, it took Peter by surprise. "Yes, Lord, you know that I love you," as if to say, "Of course I love you; you should know that." Peter was right. Jesus did know Peter's heart. He knew where his heart had been, where it was in that moment, and where it would be in the future. So, why ask the question three times? I can promise you this was not for Jesus's benefit. This was for Peter.

Peter's answers to these three questions are consistent, kind, and humbling. "You know all things, Lord." How humble is that? There is no doubt in my mind that Peter adored Jesus. In his heart of hearts, he believed he would follow him into death. It's the kind of death that I think Peter got hung up on.

DENIAL

How do you follow the son of the living God for three years, learn at his feet, watch him perform one miracle after another, only to abandon him when it matters? Well, in a word, pride. Peter was ready to go into battle for Jesus. He believed that in that battle he would die for his Messiah. How do we know this? Well, when they came to arrest Jesus, Peter was the first to throw down.

He was ready. This was the time. "I got your back, Jesus. They won't take us alive." This is what a prideful heart feels—honor, loyalty, commitment, striving to the bitter end and a noble death. Prideful hearts struggle with surrender, vulnerability, and helplessness. At Jesus's trial, Peter denied him three times. How did he go from cutting off a man's ear to denying he even knew the man at his trial? In a word, pride.

If ever you needed a friend to stand up on your behalf, it would be at your trial. Not Peter. He acquired a selective form of amnesia. Peter subscribed to the *Butch Cassidy and the Sundance Kid* methodology for leaving the planet. Go out with a bang, not with a fizzle. Peter wanted no part of surrender or humiliation. Pride doesn't give you a great deal of room for that.

Where does our pride get the best of our truth? When pride stands in the way of the truth, everyone loses. Don't get me wrong. I would have been just as terrified as Peter was in those circumstances. Cowering in some cave, I'm sure I wouldn't have had the courage to be at his trial. God understands our fears, whether they're fears about death or pain or abandonment or inadequacy.

What Jesus wanted Peter to understand in the midst of his questions was, *Because you love me, Peter, I place you in charge of that which I cherish the most, those I leave behind.* God has given that same charge to each of us. In the shadow of the cross, we are all charged with the same responsibility that Jesus gave to Peter—to feed his sheep.

As Christians, we live in a time when sharing our faith with others is met with ridicule, humiliation, and in some cases legal suits. Regardless, we have been given the great commission to go unto all the world and make disciples of men. We are not to be afraid, for we were chosen to do this by an almighty God whose love ensures that each of us is good enough.

REDEEMED

What must it have felt like for Peter to be confronted by Jesus after the resurrection? I cannot fathom the shame and guilt he must have endured in that moment. Not much is written in the Gospel account about their reunion after Jesus's resurrection. I imagine that something similar to the account in Luke 5:8 ("When Simon Peter saw this, he fell at Jesus' knees and said, 'Go away from me, Lord; I am a sinful man!'") more than likely transpired.

I have had my own number of face down, on my knees moments with God, and the thought of being in the presence of Jesus leaves me with only that reaction. I am certain of one thing that transpired between Jesus and Peter in that moment. Peter's pride was no more. Never again would his pride stand between him and his savior. Peter went on to do just what Jesus said he would. He became the foundational figure for the early church. A moment of brokenness, denying a friend, a teacher, shattered this strong-willed man's heart. Being redeemed by his savior replaced his pride with purpose.

Jesus had spoken of this shift in Peter. "Very truly I tell you, when you were younger you dressed yourself and went where you wanted; but when you are old you will stretch out your hands, and someone else will dress you and lead you where you do not want to go" (John 21:18–19 NIV). In this passage, Jesus speaks of Peter's prideful, self-seeking youth. He also illuminates how different he will be in the end.

I know what it is to be prideful and how it can rob you of God's purpose for your life. Peter is an example given to all of us of how God can use pride to change our hearts and the course of history.

For us, swallowing our pride can lead to becoming better husbands, better wives, better parents, and better friends. For Peter, swallowing his pride facilitated the creation of the early church.

In the end, Peter was a different man—no dying on the battlefield, no fighting with sword in hand. The surrender of death for Peter came long after he had surrendered his pride. There is some evidence to suggest Peter requested to be crucified on an inverted cross (Stoops 2012). In his heart, he felt unworthy of meeting his end the same way Jesus did. I am certain that at the moment of his death, the only pride he held was that he had fulfilled his purpose, for his savior, his teacher, his friend.

Key Reflections

Take a moment and consider how Peter's purpose aligns with your own:

- What are you proud of?

- Have you ever been prideful?

- Does pride make relationships more difficult?

- Do you think it was hard to love someone like Peter?

- What are some of the moments when you were most proud?

- How can God use something you're proud of for his purpose?

Chapter 9

MESSENGER

"THEREFORE, GO AND make disciples of all nations, baptizing them in the name of the Father and of the Son and of the Holy Spirit" (Matthew 28:19 NIV). Seems straightforward. These words delivered by Jesus to his disciples have become affectionately known as the great commission. I remember hearing this growing up and not thinking much about it. As I have gotten older, I find myself wrestling with the idea of making others disciples.

Who am I to make others disciples? I at one time had what could constitute a graveyard in my closet—so many skeletons you would have thought I was running one of those Halloween superstores. That's really me using inadequacy as an excuse for failing at the great commission. Perhaps the requirements for making other people disciples aren't as rigorous as I may have thought.

You are going to have to shave off another two minutes. Dad looked at me with a conflicted expression of disappointment and hope. He knew how hard I had been working but realized I was not quite there yet. It was my senior year in high school, and I had gotten a hold of a copy of the BUD/s physical fitness requirements to enter the elite Navy SEAL training program. I had nailed just about every requirement except for the 500-yard swim.

I was fortunate enough to have a pool in the backyard, but it was only ten yards long, and the transitions from one end to the other were killing me. I was convinced in open water I could do it in the 12:30 requirement.

The monotony of it was killer. I remember counting laps, breaking them up into groups of five and trying to mark my five-lap splits. Being a SEAL was a dream, something I would never achieve, but the challenge of the physical requirements appealed to me at eighteen. I knew that if I ever made it into BUD/s, the real challenge would be the mental game. I had a confidence problem, and that confidence problem is what kept me out of the SEALs.

Inadequacy is a mental sabotage that we are all guilty of. It typically comes from comparing ourselves to someone or something else. In my case, inadequacy kept me from fulfilling quite a few of my dreams. We talked about getting off our "buts" in an earlier chapter, and this ties into that concept. The "but" in any sentence is always followed by an excuse. Those excuses are rooted in some fear, often a fear of being inadequate. Excuses allow us to justify our decision to avoid something that may reveal our inadequacies.

In my experience, inadequacies fall into two categories. First, false inadequacies. These are tasks that you think you are bad at or have a weakness in, but the reality is you're just afraid to find out. For me, being a pastor has always been a false inadequacy. I have never been a pastor, nor have I ever tried. I fill in the blanks about how I would be as a pastor in an effort to protect myself from finding out the truth. The reality is I that I may be a great pastor, or I may be a horrible pastor. I would probably fall somewhere in the middle.

The second category is real inadequacies. These are those disciplines where you are just not capable. I am no basketball player. I have a real inadequacy when it comes to basketball, and that has been tested and proven over and over. On the court, I look more like a gazelle on ice than Lebron.

Is it possible that God sees our inadequacies differently than we do? Paul emphasizes weakness, which is synonymous with inadequacy in his letter to the Corinthians. "My grace is sufficient for you, for my power is made perfect in weakness" (2 Cor. 12:9 NIV). God sees our true inadequacies as a place for us to rely on him. His power is revealed in your greatest weakness when you place your trust in him instead of in yourself. The challenge is first identifying those false inadequacies and praying for courage to reveal the truth about them. In those areas you have identified inadequacies, pray for God's intervention, that his power may be revealed.

SHADOW

Ever played second fiddle to someone else? Perhaps a friend, a family member, maybe a coworker. At various points in our lives, we find ourselves in the shadow of another. In most cases, it is no fun to be in that place. Realizing that someone else shines so brightly that their presence casts a shadow on your contribution or ability can be frustrating. In other cases, it may be the most desirable place to be.

Sometimes we don't want to call attention to ourselves, for fear that others may realize just how much we lack in a certain area (aka inadequacy). I have had my fair share of moments when I would much rather be in the shadows than in the spotlight. What if the shadow you found yourself in was the shadow created by the Son of God himself?

John the Baptist was older, taller, and stranger than Jesus. Well, one of those I made up. He was related to Jesus in some way, according to Gabriel, from what we are told in the account in Luke.

> The angel answered, "The Holy Spirit will come on you, and the power of the Most High will overshadow you. So, the holy one to be born will be called the Son of God. Even Elizabeth your relative is going to have a child in her old age, and she who was said to be unable to conceive is in her sixth month. For no word from God will ever fail." (Luke 1:35–37 NIV)

John was born for one purpose; he was a messenger. His purpose was wrapped up in someone else's—and not just anyone else's. John was to pave the way for the coming of the Messiah. Think of John as a publicist, printing flyers, booking venues, all in the name of one greater than himself. He's the guy holding everything in the back, just out of view of the camera on the red carpet.

Paving the way for others is never easy. It's often thankless, exhausting, and self-deprecating work. It can and will play mind games with you. To find your purpose in being a messenger for someone else requires exceptional mental fortitude. Parents get a glimpse of this the day they find out they're pregnant.

In that instant, every decision, every dollar, every breath you take is attached to the life and purpose of another. Despite this, it can be extremely rewarding. There are plenty of movies that portray publicists and assistants as second-class citizens, used and abused until they finally have had enough. The altercations and the transitions that follow in these films are often comedic. Not John though. No fuss, no need for transition. He was happy fulfilling his purpose as Jesus's publicist—thrilled, in fact.

John was no college graduate. He had no real pedigree other than his father, Zechariah, was a priest (Luke 1:5–7). He was no prophet and did not claim to be (John 1:21). Yet he understood God's purpose for his life as one of utmost significance. Despite acknowledging he had no credentials, he baptized people to encourage repentance from sin (Matthew 3:11). His decision to become a baptizer brings him front and center to one of the most pivotal moments in Jesus's life.

The purpose we hold in God's kingdom may not always seem significant. There might be moments where you think, *How can I as an elementary school teacher affect the kingdom of God?* Perhaps you're a stay-at-home dad or mom. Often, the circles we operate in as a result of our career and life choices don't seem to have the reach we wish they would for the kingdom of God, especially when we hear about missionaries in other countries.

Keep in mind that John wasn't a missionary. He wasn't even that far from home. He did what he could for the people around him. He shared a message with those who would listen. This is something I have wrestled with much of my adult life. *I'm not witnessing enough. I'm not giving my testimony enough. I'm not bringing enough people into the kingdom.* Ask yourself this question. Is one enough?

In Matthew 3:13, when Jesus approaches John, he makes it clear what he is there to do. He's there to be baptized by John. What happens next is something I had glossed over many times—John's response to Jesus.

> But John tried to prevent him, saying, "I have need
> to be baptized by You, and do You come to me?"
> (Matthew 3:14 NASB)

I can relate but on a different level. It makes perfect sense to me that John would feel inadequate to baptize Jesus. My issues go a little deeper than that. I always thought that I am in no way qualified to bring anyone into the kingdom. John choosing to baptize Jesus, despite feeling inadequate, in that moment changed the world. One person to another altered the course of history. That one decision has driven billions of people to participate in baptism. That's the part I was missing.

The great commission isn't some sales quota you have to meet each month. It's a direction given by Jesus to each of us that starts with one conversation—a conversation that can echo into eternity for not just one person but an entire generation. Perhaps with a neighbor, a family member, or a colleague. That one conversation that plants a seed in the heart of another can make all the difference in your family, your workplace, your neighborhood, your city, and even your country. Just one conversation can have that much impact when we are talking about the saving grace of God.

John was obviously remiss about what Jesus was asking him to do. He saw himself as unworthy. Yet Jesus insisted. Talk about being conflicted. You have already admitted you are not worthy of carrying this man's sandals (Matthew 3:11), yet your reverence for this man requires you to listen and abide by his wishes. John surrenders, as he always had done, to the will of the almighty God. He baptized Jesus and gave us all a gift—an act of faith, a declaration of our salvation for all to see.

ONE VOICE

How much courage does it take to talk about your faith? In our culture, the requirement of courage has grown. Just the other day, I had a colleague tell me that Christianity will be listed as a mental disorder within the next four to six years. I said, "Well if I had to pick a mental disorder, this would be the one to have." Sometimes it's the person we are speaking to. We know how they feel about the subject, so we tend to avoid it. Other times, it's the venue. Maybe the workplace doesn't look too kindly on sharing the Gospel with others. In some cases, it's us and our lack of confidence. Regardless of the reason, it requires a level of courage to broach the subject of faith.

What was it about John that gave him the courage to share unrestrained about the coming Messiah, a claim that at the time could have gotten him thrown in jail or worse? He wasn't attached to the outcome, something I am guilty of when talking to people about Jesus. I get so wrapped up in the leading someone to Christ part that I don't give God enough room to work. When I finally let go of the outcome of sharing my faith with others, I placed it in God's hands. My emphasis needed to be on my walk and my example rather than on how persuasive I can be.

When you emphasize the relationship you have with God, the conversation you have with others becomes riddled with his love for each of us. As others see your life begin to change because of your commitment to God, anxiety replaced with peace, fear replaced with confidence, depression replaced with joy, they want what you have. Each of us is just one voice crying out in the wilderness, just like John. His walk is what drew people to him, and your walk will draw people to you.

WILD MAN

I find it remarkable how clever God is. It's almost predictable that God will use the most unconventional methods to accomplish his purpose. It's a prevalent theme throughout each character profile in this book. Wandering murderer to liberate his people. Shepherd boy to become king to his people. Crazy wild man wandering the wilderness eating bugs and honey to usher in the arrival of his one and only son.

It reminds me of *Indiana Jones and the Last Crusade*, the final scene when Indy must choose the right cup. He chooses the most ordinary, bland, unassuming cup in the room. It's an example of where Hollywood got something right. God can use anyone or anything for his purpose. He prefers to use the subtle and meek for his plans. John was the poster boy for meek. I'm sure many saw him as a madman. Camelhair shirts are not exactly in style now, nor were they back then. Yet, what does Jesus say about this wild man?

> Truly, I say to you, among those born of women there has arisen no one greater than John the Baptist. Yet the one who is least in the kingdom of heaven is greater than he. (Matthew 11:11 ESV)

Uh, no one greater? Ever? Not David, not Moses? Surely Elijah. Imagine being recognized in such a way by the son of God, the Messiah.

"Finally, out of the shadow and into the spotl ..."

"Oops."

"Wait a minute. What did he say?"

"That last part, what was that?"

"The least in heaven is greater than me?"

"Man, just when I thought I had arrived, cut me down again."

This would have been my reaction. But not John's. John was thrilled that he had been chosen as the messenger, that his existence was the catalyst that announced the salvation of humankind. John provides us an example of how our purpose may not always be glamorous but is always critical. We have something that John didn't have the rest of the story. John was born into the shadow of Jesus, but we were all born in the light of the cross.

Key Reflections

Take a moment to consider John's position in the historic account of Jesus's life and how it relates to your purpose in God's kingdom:

- Have you ever felt like you were in the shadow of another?

- How does inadequacy rob you of the purpose God has for your life?

- Is sharing your faith something you feel comfortable doing?

- Share your faith with someone who is also a believer and see what suggestions they have about sharing with nonbelievers.

Chapter 10
WRONG

W HAT DOES IT mean to have a pedigree? We typically hear the term used when referring to animals. Dogs, horses, even pigeons have pedigrees. It's a set of documents and characteristics that provide us with a foundation of the origins and history of that which is pedigreed.

In the case of dogs, a pedigree gives us a lineage of the animal's family. This provides us with a sense of understanding about what we can expect from dogs as they get older and what kind of traits their children are likely to carry forward. For many people and industries, pedigree is a big deal. We have pedigrees. Each and every one of us. Ours are a little different.

Typically, our pedigrees are referred to as our ancestry. I do believe there is a delineation between pedigree and ancestry. When you think of the pedigree of a person, you think of not only the stock with which they came but also their achievements—where they went to college, who they married, what job they have, their awards and certificates. Pedigree doesn't just emphasize the positive. Some pedigrees have quite a degree of negative in them—say, the pedigree of a serial killer. Regardless of the individual, we all have pedigrees. Some of what exists in our pedigree is driven by how we think.

How we feel is defined by how we think. Take a moment and unpack that. Think of an ex-boyfriend or ex-girlfriend where the relationship ended in a bad way. As you are thinking about them, how do you feel? Now think about someone you love. How quickly did your feelings change? We respond to music in a similar fashion. Some songs conjure thoughts of happiness, and our mood follows. Some country song can come on the radio, and you pull to the side of the road because you can't see through the puddle of tears welling up in your eyes.

This was the case for me and my Christian walk. How I thought about my walk with Christ and the good and bad decisions I made drove me to this place of not being worthy to bring people into the kingdom of God, like my pedigree was tarnished. I felt as if my capabilities as a Christian didn't make the cut for making other people followers. If I could just shave a few sins off my life, polish my pedigree a little, then I would be a good candidate for the great commission. My concern was people would see where I fell short and then accuse me of being a hypocrite. I kept thinking, *I just need to get my walk perfect, and then I can start bringing people to Christ.*

THE JONESES

Pedigrees are made up of credentials. Our culture is dominated by credentials, so much so we hardly think about it directly. Sure, we are always interested in what people do for a living, where they went to school, and how many kids they have, but is it really a personal interest or is there something more to these probing questions?

The questions we ask the Joneses allow us to place them into categories, which provides us the ability to generate a comparison to our own lives. The credentials don't end there. What kind of car do they drive? How big is their house? How big is the rock on her finger?

These questions have answers, and all these answers give us a view into the credentials that person has. Many of us are trying to keep up. We work longer hours. We get our kids into private schools. We upgrade our car, our house, our wedding ring. Why? Because we want others to see our credentials—without bragging, that is. Because that's just rude.

Is it any surprise that when we look at our faith walk, we do similar things? Are we as active in the church? Do we pray as much? Are our prayers as good as the pastor's? Let's host the neighborhood group at our house. I call this "keeping up with the righteous." As Christians, we have secular credentials and Christian credentials. Soon, your Christian credentials become intertwined with your secular credentials. Now keeping up with the Joneses becomes keeping up with the holy Joneses. Often these two concepts clash.

Secular credentials don't always look good on your Christian résumé and vice versa. How do we master the need for having credentials in our culture and fulfill the great commission? The answer begins with putting Christ over credentials.

RIGHTEOUS

What would it take for you to change your name? What does your name mean to you? What's wrapped up in your name? Your identity. We talked about names back in chapter 5. Esther had to change her name, which appeared to support her dual citizenship as a Hebrew living under Persian rule. My mother gave me my name. It's a gift, one of the first we receive.

People change names for many reasons. Sometimes it's to become something, and sometimes it's to forget something. The author of the majority of the New Testament went through a similar change, changing his name from Saul to Paul. I think it's important to delineate between who Saul and Paul were. I might be so bold as to engender the idea that they were different enough to merit a change in name—dramatically different enough to be considered different people occupying the same person. Saul's mission was to fulfill every aspect of the Mosaic law and tradition—to use his words, "a Hebrew among Hebrews" (Phil. 3:5).

Saul is a compelling figure—dynamic, charismatic, pensive, and educated, a scholar and a dual citizen, both a Jew and a Roman. If you consider the pedigree of Saul, it becomes clear the unique position he holds. His entire life, every choice he ever made would become the driving force behind his purpose.

Saul was a Pharisee (Phil. 3:5). He was voraciously committed to the almighty God, the God of Abraham, Isaac, and Jacob. No doubt he could recite to you every commandment, and I'm not just referring to the ten on the stone. I'm talking about the 613 found in the books of the Old Testament. His purpose was to be a godly man and facilitate that endeavor in the lives of others, by whatever means necessary.

Righteousness is a difficult pursuit. Many have tried and failed. What we understand of Saul is that he was blameless (Phil. 3:6). We also know he was willing to forsake everything to quiet this Jesus rebellion no matter the cost. *These so-called Christians must be eradicated before they bring God's wrath upon us all. If you won't relent, then torture and death are reserved for you.* Saul, the man who will one day become the spokesperson for all of Christianity, is a Christian killer. He presides over Stephen's stoning and even condones it (Acts 7:58; 9:1). He has found his purpose—to eliminate the blight that this Jesus of Nazareth has brought to his world, even if he has to travel to far corners of the world to do so.

I cannot underscore enough the mission and purpose that Saul saw in the eradication of Christianity. He would use every resource, every tool in his arsenal to that end. There's one small problem. What if Saul's purpose is all wrong? How do you know if it's right or wrong? What does it feel like to be wrong?

RIGHT AND WRONG

"What does it feel like to be wrong?" This question had a succinct and rapid answer. "It feels terrible." Then the speaker clarified. "I didn't ask what it feels like when you realize you are wrong but when you are wrong." She quickly followed with additional support for her real question. Kathryn Schultz was giving a TED talk on being wrong. This seminar provided details from her book *Being Wrong: Adventures in the Margin of Error.* She challenged me and the audience, along with millions of YouTubers, to truly consider what it means to be wrong. Her challenge to all of us is simple: doesn't being wrong feel very much like being right?

It's an interesting argument, one that is difficult to refute. It is worth noting the irony wrapped up in this intellectual venture of right and wrong. Being asked the question of what it feels like to be wrong leads you down the path of realizing that your answer to the question, assuming it is like mine, is wrong and always has been.

Kathryn's argument is that only when we realize that we are wrong do the negative emotions begin to overwhelm our mind. I began to think about ideas and thoughts I had when I was growing up that were solidified as right in my mind but turned out to be wrong.

My favorite memory for this endeavor is song lyrics. My daughter, "Fuego," as she has become affectionately known, would sing, "Hold me close, Tony Danza," to the classic song "Tiny Dancer" by Elton John and was convinced those were the lyrics. Imagine her disappointment when she found out that this beguiling melody was not about an intimate embrace with everybody's favorite housekeeper but somehow describes the grip of a ballerina? To this day, whenever the song comes on the radio, you will find the whole family being led in chorus to "Tony Danza."

Songs are just one of many areas I get wrong. I remember *Dilbert* creator Scott Adams in an interview speaking about challenging complacency. He spoke of Elon Musk and Steve Jobs as modern-day examples. He spoke of how there are people in history who stop and look at our daily lives and ask the question, "What if we are doing it wrong?"

Complacency is an interesting phenomenon. Humans are hardwired to establish stable and secure routines. Some of us have our wires connected a little differently. We are driven to challenge the routine. Galileo, Edison, King, and many others throughout our history have challenged not just our daily lives but our way of thinking.

Challenging the status quo is often met with resistance and criticism. For some reason, it is difficult to rip the "we've always done it that way" from our cold, dead synapses. As I mentioned before, I can't even get my daughter to stop singing "Tony Danza." Why are we so driven to routine?

Sociologists will tell you that habit and routine provide us with a sense of security and stability. This is a basis for our primal needs as humans. The rules and norms we place upon ourselves and our society are there to enhance our ability to thrive. Seems contradictory. If we are thriving, why the need for new ideas and new inventions?

Thriving doesn't always mean that your habits and routines are the most effective or the most efficient. Creativity and thriving go hand in hand. When we thrive, we become more creative. It's when our routine and habits are out of concert that we have little time or energy to create or adopt new ideas or patterns. Something in our wiring tells us to solve our current state, and then we can adopt, create, and explore new habits or routines.

Let's consider an example. My wife and I bought a car a few months ago. We knew nothing about the manufacturer or the car, to be quite honest. We knew it was all electric, and that was appealing to us—no gas, no oil changes, cheap registration, and license plates that get us into the HOV lane. We had never owned an all-electric car and had never owned a car by this manufacturer.

The first few days were challenging. I had always driven Fords. Let me tell you, this car was no Ford. I couldn't figure out how to turn the car on or off. Turns out there is no on or off. *Where are the headlights, windshield wipers, cruise control?* I had no idea how to drive this car, even though I have been driving cars for the better part of thirty years. Despite my driving record, the learning curve had started over as it related to these driver tasks. The manufacturer of this car had an ever so slightly different way of handling each of them, compared to what I was used to.

As a result, my senses were heightened, my driving more conservative. Tasks like turning on my turn signal were less of an afterthought and a more deliberate action. Someone messed with my habits, my stuff got moved, my routine was interrupted. Regardless of the change in routine or habit, when these things happen, our mind is forced to go through a mental shift that for many of us is uncomfortable.

Now take this trivial example of a buying an unfamiliar car and impose on it something more dramatic—loss of a job, a loved one, a spouse. How do these life events alter our routines? Dramatically to say the least. Many that find themselves in any one of these situations, they find it difficult to go on, let alone thrive. Each of these tragedies alters our routines, forcing us to go off autopilot and attempt to grab the wheel. Sometimes it's not the loss of someone or something that shocks us out of our state of comfortable bliss. Sometimes it's when we realize that what we've done or are doing is wrong.

SPIRIT SHOCK

One of my favorite movies of all time stars one of my favorite actors of all time. The movie is *Grosse Pointe Blank,* and the actor is John Cusack. For those of you who haven't seen it, I encourage you to put this book down somewhere safe. Carve out the next one hour and forty-seven minutes to immerse yourself in what has to be one of the greatest cinematic Cusack performances of all time. You will not regret this endeavor, I can assure you. (Dramatic pause for effect.)

Welcome back! Now that you have been exposed to the pinnacle of Cusack's canon, we can proceed with confidence that both you and I are seeing the world through the same lens. Remember the diner scene? Minnie Driver proceeds to tell John what he needs.

Debi: You know what you need?

Marty: What?

Debi: Shockabuku.

Marty: You wanna tell me what that means?

Debi: It's a swift, spiritual kick to the head that alters your reality forever.

Marty: Oh, that'd be good. I think.

Yes, shockabuku. It is one of the many nuggets of wisdom that has stayed with me all these years. *A swift spiritual kick to the head that alters your reality forever.* I am not entirely sure that this word is rooted in any other facet of culture outside of the masterpiece that is *Grosse Pointe Blank.* Nevertheless, it is appropriate to each of us for the following reasons.

Either you have experienced such a thing as a shockabuku, or you are in desperate need of one. Regardless of the category you fall into, the term is beneficial.

Spirit shock, as I like to call it, is that moment when God does an intervention in your life. The best example I can provide is Job 38 and 39. Job went through a rather dramatic spirit shock when confronted with God's response to his preceding laundry list of verses that asked, "Why me?" I still think the author of that book should have put *mic drop* somewhere at the end of God's response to Job.

I have had several spirit shocks in my life, and they always do the same thing—help me realize why I am not God and why he is God. It's a humbling experience, followed by an overwhelming understanding of just how much love, mercy, and compassion God has for the idiot that I was prior to his coming-to-Jesus talk with me. No pun intended.

Job's not the only one who went through this experience. Jonah, David, Peter—virtually anyone who came to terms with God's purpose and plan encountered a spirit shock. There is, however, one person whose shock didn't just affect his spirit; it became the catalyst for the beginning of an entire spiritual revolution.

BLIND

I've never been blind. I cannot imagine living in a world of darkness. I'm a visual person and always have been. I like to look at beautiful things. Blindness doesn't always come in the form of darkness, at least not physical darkness. Sometimes we are blinded by love or blinded to the truth, as is the case with Saul.

Saul gets the spirit shock award. Transitioning from Christian killer to Christian creator virtually overnight can only be attributed to the type of spirit shock that shakes the foundation of one's identity. In the case of Saul, this shock was so bright it left him blind.

Saul's emphasis had always been on a person's actions—their pursuit of the law or lack thereof, their commitment to God and all his commandments. Saul was so focused on the physical he couldn't see the truth in the heart of each man, the very emphasis Christ came to underscore.

Saul was so blind to it he dismissed the followers of Christ without ever once examining their hearts. When confronted by Christ, his sight was taken from him, the one thing that was distracting him and perpetuating his self-driven purpose of eradicating Christians. God had a new purpose for Saul—not as Saul but as Paul.

Paul is credited with writing the majority of the New Testament. He seems the most unlikely candidate for the job, but if you dig deep, who better to facilitate the tenets of Christianity than a Roman Jew? His dual citizenship afforded him the ability to address Jews and Gentiles alike. His notoriety provided him the means to speak in venues where others would not dare. Paul's scholarship enabled him to write to cities all over the known world, addressing the many challenges of infant Christianity. All of this makes Paul an excellent candidate for becoming early Christianity's publicist. But there's more, as there always is when we become the key to unlocking God's purpose for our lives.

UNFORGIVEN

I struggle with being forgiven. It's hard sometimes to accept forgiveness. Sometimes it's only natural to want to be punished and yelled at for the things we've done wrong. I am bad at accepting forgiveness. I feel unworthy when my family forgives me. I see it as a burden they must bear as a result of my failings as a husband and father. You can imagine my struggle with God's forgiveness. We know all the stuff we've done and even worse the stuff we've thought. It's all unfiltered and raw and messy. How can a righteous God forgive us for such things? Enter Paul.

Perhaps you have encountered this situation witnessing to someone. They share with you that they believe God will not accept them because their history is too torrid. Maybe they're convinced there is absolutely no way God could see past the things they have done—drugs, violence, affairs, and a laundry list of other things that they rattle off like barricades stacked against the door to keep Jesus out, as if to say, "Jesus, if you want to forgive me, you have to wade through all my wickedness."

Paul's story allows us to assure them that these sins they keep piling up in God's way have already been seen, heard, and accounted for. They're gone. They were gone before they were thought of or done. Regardless of how many they offer, no matter if each one is more wicked than the other, the truth remains. God's forgiveness never fails. Sometimes, witnessing to others comes down to the question, What is the worst sin someone could commit?

Most people arrive at murder. Paul is no stranger to murder. He considered himself the worst of all sinners (1 Tim 1:15). Not just any murder, the murder of a young man who was a follower of Christ (Acts 8:1). The man responsible for writing most of the New

Testament not only killed people but killed Christians, for no other reason than being Christian.

God's promise of forgiveness and salvation is irrefutable. He offers this promise to both the righteous and the wicked. Despite our crimes, our sins, God offers a gift to each of us that Paul learned firsthand—a promise Paul penned for the church in Rome and a promise we can be confidant of today. Romans 8:38–39, explains it perfectly:

> For I am convinced that neither death nor life, neither angels nor demons, neither the present nor the future, nor any powers, neither height nor depth, nor anything else in all creation, will be able to separate us from the love of God that is in Christ Jesus our Lord.

Nothing separates us from God's love—not our blockade of sin, wickedest thought, or most heinous deed. When we realize this promise is not just for the best of us but also available for the worst of us, we are immediately confronted with the question, Why? The answer is simple, and it is the same answer to the question of why God does anything. That he may be glorified. God not only forgave Paul; he made him his spokesperson. If God can forgive Paul for all he did, he can and has forgiven us.

> For my own sake, for my own sake, I do this. How can I let myself be defamed? I will not yield my glory to another. (Isaiah 48:11 NIV)

Key Reflections

Take a moment to consider Paul's transformation:

- Are there areas of your life where you have been wrong and didn't know it?

- Are there friends or family members who are wrong about you?

- When was the last time you were wrong? How do you feel about being wrong?

- Are there things you think about yourself that are wrong?

- What transformations do you feel God is putting you through to become the key to unlocking your purpose for his kingdom?

Chapter 11
LOVE

I REMEMBER SEEING THE picture for the first time. A young boy, maybe two or three, sat on wooden chair in an army uniform. The picture was faded but well loved as it sat stoically on the top of the piano. Not much older than three myself, I moved closer to this image of a young boy and immediately was overtaken with envy of such an awesome uniform. *What is that boy wearing? Where did he get such an outfit? Why don't I have that outfit? Who is this person? Maybe I can borrow this uniform.*

I ran to my grandmother, picture in hand, and asked about the young boy in the photograph. She smiled gently and said, "That's your father when he was just about your age." My mind exploded.

With confusion on my face, I blurted out, "My father was little? Huh. What happened to him? Will I stop being little? Why is he holding out on me on this whole uniform thing?"

My grandmother proceeded to tell me about how right after that picture was taken, she found him flying around the living room. I was in disbelief. My dad flying around the living room. *Must be the uniform.*

When my dad was two, he had told my grandmother that he was going to be a pilot. My grandfather was a navy pilot in World War II, and having been born right at the beginning of the war, my dad was enthralled with all things aeronautic.

When he had his tonsils out, he fought with the nurses, avoiding the sleepy gas by kicking, screaming, and even holding his breath. My grandmother walked in the room and said to him, "Jay, listen. I think there's an airplane overhead." He immediately stopped his defense, looked up toward the ceiling, took a deep breath, and went to sleep.

My dad loved airplanes. He loved flying and was willing to do anything to become a pilot. He once told me about a farmer who lived down the road from his parents' farm and had a biplane. From the time he was sixteen, he spent every hour he could at the farmer's house, trying to get rides in that airplane. His first ride, he was even more hooked. His purpose was solidified in an instant. He was going to be a pilot.

My dad went on to a career in the US Air Force and then flew commercial airliners, totaling over forty years of flying airplanes. His passion for flying drove him to do whatever it took to fly planes. He gave up quite a bit to become a fighter pilot. Pilot training in the USAF is an extremely selective process. At one time, for every hundred students that applied, only one graduated.

Despite these odds, my dad managed to graduate from pilot training in 1965. He was singularly focused on flying planes and serving his country in the process. My dad volunteered for Vietnam, and after his first tour, he requested to go back again. He was a dedicated man and committed to his purpose.

I, on the other hand, bounced from degree to degree in college. I went from job to job and eventually ended up in a career that was killing me slowly and all for the wrong reasons.

I landed a job at a major telecommunications company doing database development work. Great company, good values but stressful work. On call nights and weekend, it was a challenging job that took a lot out of me. My dad always said, "Find what makes you happy and then find a way to get paid for it." For him, that was flying. For me, that was ... I have no idea.

Finding purpose comes naturally for some. For others, it's a daily battle filled with emptiness and inadequacy. I have met so many who have found their purpose by accident. Many have said, "If two years ago someone had told me I would be doing this today, I would have said they were crazy."

Moses found his purpose late in his life. Peter found his purpose in the death of his pride. For those of us who struggle with purpose, like many of the profiles in this book did, it's evident that God's timing and intervention are required to reveal our purpose. If that's the case, and we know these two things are in God's court, then what part do we play?

PATIENCE

It's almost cliché at this point. Patience is an exhausted subject in our culture, especially within the Christian community. Despite how we as a culture frame or manipulate the concept of patience, the fact that we have written volumes on the subject is an indication of its necessity in our lives. Patience is not the issue. It's the opposite of patience that is our issue. That said, the antithesis of patience should be the focus of our discussion—anxiousness.

We are all born with anxiousness. Put a cake in front of a baby and watch them hyperventilate with excitement. The response of that child to that cake is one of anxiousness. My twelve-year-old cannot wait for thirteen, sixteen, college, the FBI, marriage, kids— the list goes on and on. What makes us anxious? The answer is simple: experience.

We are all experience junkies, wired that way from birth. The friends we have, the things we buy, the people we marry are all driven by a desire for experience. Our culture has made a mint on experience. Every theme park, shopping mall, social media site, smartphone, and even church has capitalized on the deeply rooted desire for experience.

Anxiousness is driven by the desire for the next experience. Consider how connected temptation is to anxiousness. Temptation is nothing more than the fear of a missed opportunity. Should I have dessert or not? Do I claim this on my taxes or not? Should I have that affair? All these questions come as a result of weighing our options. We are anxious and curious about the experience and afraid of missing out if we choose to say no. How do we unpack this? As always, God's intention seems like the best place to start.

Experience, and all the glory that is wrapped up in it, is God's design. Regardless of the subject, the ability to experience anything is designed and intended by God. All your senses, all your emotions, every fiber of your being is designed by God for experience. When you bite into a warm, sweet, delicious piece of apple pie, that sensation is God ordained and God designed.

This should come as no surprise. God creates stuff. God creates humanity. God says to humanity, "Enjoy my stuff." Through God-designed and -ordained experiences, he reveals his glory and nature to us. If you ever had my grandmother's apple pie, you would know the fullness of God's glory.

These abilities we are given are God's mechanisms for us to experience him in every aspect of our existence, through his spirit that he has placed in all things. It's no wonder we all seek experience. Whether it's apple pie, skydiving, or curling up with a good book and a hot cup of coffee, each moment of our lives is permeated with the element of experience and the nature of our creator.

Satan is not without his own intentions for experience. He wants your experiences to be filled with things that distract you from God's purpose. Greed, lust, anger, selfishness. Each of them is Satan's manipulation of God's intention. In *The Pursuit of God*, A.W. Tozer expresses it this way: "But sin has introduced complications and has made those very gifts of God a potential source of ruin to the soul."

God wanted us to have abundance. There was more in the Garden of Eden than Adam and Eve could ever have needed. Solomon had acquired more wealth than we can comprehend. The trick Satan played is when he made us believe we should hoard our abundance and acquire more only to keep more for ourselves.

God intended intimacy to be a connection between a husband and wife, something they shared uniquely with each other and no one else.

Satan led us to believe that sex is nothing more than a casual sport. God intended anger for us to identify that which is unjust and unrighteous. Satan uses it to rob us of our joy.

God designed humans with the ability to identify their own needs and fulfill them through his provision. Satan took that sense of self and led us to believe we are the only thing that matters.

The intention of God for all our experiences and the manipulation of Satan within those things have always been present. What separates them is us.

Our choices regarding experience and temptation matter. In chapter 5, we saw how opportunity, anxiousness, and temptation almost led to the undoing of a king. I often wonder how God might have blessed David had he felt the temptation of Bathsheba and decided to go play Xbox instead.

Anxiousness is a sign in the moment that we need God's consultation. This is by design. God wanted us to realize that by seeking him in the moment of our excitement and anxiousness about an experience or opportunity, his blessings will abound in ways we cannot fathom.

This is about building our relationship with God. He has designed us in such a way that we can stumble on our own or be blessed by his love and grace. Regardless of the steps you take, God will always be there to celebrate your victory or comfort you in your loss.

> I say to myself, "The Lord is my portion; therefore, I will wait for him." The Lord is good to those whose hope is in him, to the one who seeks him; it is good to wait quietly for the salvation of the Lord. (Lament. 3:24–26 NIV)

STEEL

So often, I have heard of people being compared to clay. The imagery of a potter molding and shaping clay has come to signify the relationship of God changing us, shaping us into what we should be. I don't know about you, but I am not clay. Iron, steel, titanium, and diamond seem more appropriate elements to characterize my substance and how resistant I am to change.

Getting me to change my heart requires a great deal of heat and a whole lot of cutting and pounding. Most of the people I know are the same. Consider the characters in this book and what it took to change them. Nothing graceful about how Moses or Paul changed. Quite honestly, I don't see any of them changing in the absence of something dramatic and earth-shattering.

We are all resistant to change. I know some will argue that they are change agents, happy and willing to change, no tragedy necessary. Changing your heart to become what God needs you to be is always dramatic. Even those who change gradually would tell you that the alteration, albeit slow, was dramatic.

God's part is the earth-shattering wake-up call that shows us the exact shape of our heart. Our part is having a heart that's willing to take on a new shape.

In our culture, our hearts are beaten and broken with a relentless barrage of not good enough and betrayal. It is a vicious cycle of making ourselves vulnerable to the world around us, only to be taken advantage of, mocked, and ridiculed.

I hear story after story of people from every demographic being hurt by friends, family, and strangers. The betrayals mount, the rejections overwhelm, and the fear takes hold. The mind begins to put protections in place. *I'll never let anyone in ever again. No one will hurt me like that again. I can't trust anyone anymore.* Each of these thoughts hardens our hearts and places us on a path of keeping everyone and everything at arm's length.

Heartache is equal opportunity; it does not discriminate who it goes after. There are so many avenues to be vulnerable today. Our personal lives have never been so available to the world. Consider that when you jump onto social media, you are sharing your life with the world. Family, friends, jobs, hobbies, passions, thoughts—all these things end up on social media in one way or another. Don't look now, but that's your heart you are putting out there for the world to see and criticize.

The desire to share what's in our hearts is God designed and God ordained. He has a plan for that as well. He is desperate to hear your heart in every breath you breathe, every smile that crosses your face, and every tear you cry.

We share our hearts and expose ourselves to people we don't even know, and when those people aren't prepared for what we have in us, we all get hurt, whether it's envy, jealousy, greed, lust, or rage that drives us to words and actions intended to break down and humiliate. The outcome for all involved is never good.

Our part, in purpose, comes down to our ability to let God do the work. Surrendering the deepest part of yourself to a God that asks for your faith and your trust can be the hardest thing you will do in your life, especially after a lifetime of watching others destroy the most beautiful parts of who you are.

Your heart is a gift from God, and its condition matters to him. Take your heart off social media and start putting it in God's hands and see the changes that can happen.

HOPE

What does it mean to have hope? What does it look like? If someone had it, could you tell? In chapter 2, we talked about God's intention for humanity. We also talked about how our freedom revealed to us our need for a redeemer. Our choices made the difference between walking with God and wandering in the wilderness. Despite our choices, however wicked or wonderful they are, God refused to be without us. He did the one thing that would bridge the chasm we created between our hearts and his.

Jesus's purpose has been the subject of many pieces of literature throughout history. Consider knowing your purpose the way Jesus knew his, living a life devoted to one outcome. Nothing can distract you—no static, no noise. Created and crafted for a single mission. I often consider the cost of such a life and am quickly reminded that with the cost came the greatest reward in human history—salvation.

The beauty in the design of our path to salvation is one that only a creator of unbounding love could have conjured. Jesus, born a man, lived to die for the sins of the world. Born, but why? Why not just form him like he did Adam? Have him preach the Gospel, share the good news, convey the tenets of the new covenant, carry out the sacrifice, and be done with it.

Timing played a role even in Jesus's purpose. A loving God wouldn't do that. A loving God says, "I will share this life with you. I will experience as you have experienced. I will suffer the way you suffer. I will meet you right where you are. From crawling to walking, from adolescence to all the joys of puberty. From learning the cost of friendship and family to feeling the loss of a loved one." God said, "I will do it all so that you may know I understand." There is patience in this story of the son of God. With God's purpose, timing matters, and as with Jesus, his timing is always best.

Jesus emphasized the condition of a person's heart. This was his biggest point of contention with the Pharisees. We see this clearly in the parable of the Pharisee and the tax collector.

> Two men went up to the temple to pray, one a Pharisee and the other a tax collector. The Pharisee stood by himself and prayed: 'God, I thank you that I am not like other people—robbers, evildoers, adulterers—or even like this tax collector. I fast twice a week and give a tenth of all I get.' But the tax collector stood at a distance. He would not even look up to heaven, but beat his breast and said, 'God, have mercy on me, a sinner.' (Luke 18:10-13 NIV)

The emphasis of this story is not on the accolades, accomplishments, or purity of either man but on the condition of their hearts. This story is one that resonates with me more than others. I have been both Pharisee and tax collector in my life, and I know the condition my heart was in, in both circumstances. In one, a heart of stone closed off to the world and to God. In the other, on my knees, my heart in pieces as an offering to the one who made me.

Jesus knew that God's purpose for any person began in their heart, and he spent his ministry challenging others to see that. He provided the example of what condition our hearts must be in for God to use us in his kingdom—not perfect, not unblemished, but surrendered and offered to the only one who can mend what each of us has shattered.

It's no secret the purpose the son of God fulfilled, the choice he made to surrender a perfect and unblemished heart for the sake of the world. It's evident, in all we know about the life of Jesus, that his purpose was set the day he was born, a purpose that each of us was made for. From Adam and Eve to the baby who just now took its first breath, our purpose, our place in this world is no different from that of the savior of this world, a shared purpose each of us has and is wired for—a purpose to forgive, a purpose to restore, and a purpose to love.

References

Eckstein, D., K. J. Aycock, M. A. Sperber, J. McDonald, V. Van Wiesner III, R. E. Watts, and P. Ginsburg. 2010. "A Review of 200 Birth-Order Studies: Lifestyle Characteristics." *Journal of Individual Psychology*. Retrieved October 13, 2017, from https://utpress.utexas.edu/journals/journal-of-individual-psychology.

Freedman, R. 1983. David. "Woman, a Power Equal to Man." *Biblical Archaeology Review* 9, no. 1: 56–58.

Martin, SJ James. Dec. 18, 2015. "Opinion | Mother Teresa, about to Be Named a Saint, Felt Terrible Pain 'of God Not Wanting Me.'" *Washington Post*. www.washingtonpost.com/news/acts-of-faith/wp/2015/12/18/mother-teresa-about-to-be-sainted-felt-terrible-pain-of-god-not-wanting-me/?noredirect=on&utm_term=.a898e13e0a52.

Rabinowicz, T. 1994. *A Guide to Life: Jewish Laws and Customs of Mourning*. Northvale, NJ: J. Aronson.

Stoops, Robert F., and Julian Victor Hills. 2012. *The Acts of Peter.* Polebridge Press.

Walton, John H. 2001. *The NIV Application Commentary Genesis.* Zondervan.

Printed in the United States
By Bookmasters